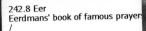

EERDMANS' BOOK OF

FAMOUS PRAYERS

COMPILED BY VERONICA ZUNDEL

William B. Eerdmans Publishing Company
Grand Rapids, Michigan

Copyright © 1983 Lion Publishing

First American edition published 1984
through special arrangement with Lion
by Wm. B. Eerdmans Publishing Company,
255 Jefferson Ave. S.E., Grand Rapids,
Michigan 49503

ISBN 0-8028-3593-7

Reprinted 1984

Printed and bound in Hong Kong by
Mandarin Offset International (HK) Ltd

Special thanks to the Rev. Geoff van der Weegen
for his invaluable help in collecting the prayers

Illustrations

Contents

Introduction

'Teach us to pray', Jesus' disciples asked their master; and in reply he gave them not a list of rules, but a specimen prayer. It was a wise answer, for we learn mainly by example and imitation. Talking to God, like all communication, has to be learned. We are apt to let our thoughts wander or get lost in speculation. At times we try to impress God with the length of our prayers or the holiness of our sentiments, forgetting that he sees into our hearts.

Using prayers composed by others can help to focus our minds on God and remind us of what prayer is all about. Sometimes, like the lover who reads poems to his beloved, we may find that someone else's words express our feelings more clearly than we ourselves can.

This book is an attempt to gather some of the most enduring and best-loved prayers used by the Christian church throughout its history. They cover a wide range of human feelings and experience: joy, sorrow, guilt, thankfulness, need, compassion, self-surrender, brotherhood. Some have famous authors; some are anonymous, passed down from generation to generation. They were prayed by monks in cloisters and soldiers in battlefields, by individuals and congregations, by those with a strong, mature faith and those whose faith was in its infancy. Their mood ranges from the despairing to the decidedly light-hearted, with more than a dash of humour.

The common factor I have looked for in making this selection is a directness and honesty which refuses to put on a pious show before God or others. In a sense we are all beginners at prayer — there are no experts. The best prayers, with which we can all identify, come out of a realization that, in St Paul's words, 'We do not know how we ought to pray, but the Spirit himself pleads with God for us.'

As with all anthologies, the reader may miss some favourite prayer from this collection. It is meant to be no more than an introduction to the vast treasury of great Christian prayers. Those who are inspired by this book will be able to look elsewhere for more prayers by the authors included here.

Above all, I hope these prayers will be read not just for literary or historical interest, but as a living stimulus to the reader's own prayers. Perhaps, too, they may be an inspiration to the writing of new prayers which will in their own turn become favourites of future generations.

Veronica Zundel

Bible Prayers

For hundreds of years the Hebrew people recorded God's dealings with them — his acts of deliverance, his words of revelation, his promises of a Saviour and a new world. Their writings, inspired by God, are found in the Bible. It is a history book, a book of wisdom, a book of laws, a hymn book. It is also a full and varied book of prayers.

God's people prayed for strength, for forgiveness, for their own daily needs and the needs of others. They cried out to God in despair; they praised and thanked him for his goodness. Their prayers have been a model for many other prayers throughout the centuries.

Praise For Creation
PSALM 8

O Lord, our Lord,
how majestic is your name
in all the earth!
You have set your glory
above the heavens.
From the lips of children and infants
you have ordained praise
because of your enemies,
to silence the foe and the avenger.
When I consider your heavens,
the work of your fingers,
the moon and the stars,
which you have set in place,
what is man that you are mindful of him,
the son of man that you care for him?

You made him a little lower than
the heavenly beings
and crowned him with glory and honour.
You made him ruler over the works
of your hands;
you put everything under his feet:
all flocks and herds,
and the beasts of the field,
the birds of the air
and the fish of the sea,
all that swim the paths of the seas.
O Lord, our Lord,
how majestic is your name
in all the earth!

A Cry For Help
PSALM 42 :1-6

As the deer pants for streams of water,
so my soul pants for you, O God.
My soul thirsts for God, for the living God.
When can I go and meet with God?
My tears have been my food day and night,
while men say to me all day long,
'Where is your God?'
These things I remember
as I pour out my soul:
how I used to go with the multitude,
leading the procession to the house of God.
with shouts of joy and thanksgiving
among the festive throng.
Why are you downcast, O my soul?
Why so disturbed within me?
Put your hope in God,
for I will yet praise him,
my Saviour and my God.

King David's Confession
FROM PSALM 51

Have mercy on me, O God,
according to your unfailing love;
according to your great compassion
blot out my transgressions.
Wash away all my iniquity
and cleanse me from my sin.
For I know my transgressions,
and my sin is always before me.
Against you, you only, have I sinned
and done what is evil in your sight,
so that you are proved right when you speak
and justified when you judge.

Surely I have been a sinner from birth,
sinful from the time my mother conceived me.
Surely you desire truth in the inner parts;
you teach me wisdom in the inmost place.
Create in me a pure heart, O God,
and renew a steadfast spirit within me.
Do not cast me from your presence
or take your Holy Spirit from me.
Restore to me the joy of your salvation
and grant me a willing spirit, to sustain me.
Then I will teach transgressors your ways
and sinners will turn back to you.

A Prayer of Trust
PSALM 131

My heart is not proud, O Lord,
my eyes are not haughty;
I do not concern myself with great matters
or things too wonderful for me.
But I have stilled and quieted my soul;
like a weaned child with its mother,
like a weaned child is my soul within me.
O Israel, put your hope in the Lord
both now and for evermore.

The Lord's Prayer
MATTHEW 6 : 9-13

Our Father in heaven,
hallowed be your name,
your kingdom come,
your will be done
on earth as it is in heaven.
Give us today our daily bread.
Forgive us our debts,
as we also have forgiven our
debtors.
And lead us not into
temptation,
but deliver us from the evil one.

Mary's Song of Praise
LUKE 1: 46-55

My soul praises the Lord
and my spirit rejoices in God my Saviour,
for he has been mindful of the humble state of his servant.
From now on all generations will call me blessed,
for the Mighty One has done great things for me —
holy is his name.
His mercy extends to those who fear him,
from generation to generation.
He has performed mighty deeds with his arm;
he has scattered those who are proud in their inmost
thoughts.
He has brought down rulers from their thrones
but has lifted up the humble.
He has filled the hungry with good things
but has sent the rich away empty.
He has helped his servant Israel,
remembering to be merciful
to Abraham and his descendants for ever,
even as he said to our fathers.

Jesus' Prayer For Deliverance
MARK 14 : 36

Abba, Father, everything is possible for you. Take this
cup from me. Yet not what I will, but what you will.

Paul's Prayer For the Ephesians
EPHESIANS 3 :14-19

I kneel before the Father, from whom the whole family in
heaven and on earth derives its name. I pray that out of
his glorious riches he may strengthen you with power
through his Spirit in your inner being, so that Christ may
dwell in your hearts through faith. And I pray that you,
being rooted and established in love, may have power,
together with all the saints, to grasp how wide and long
and high and deep is the love of Christ, and to know this
love that surpasses knowledge — that you may be filled to
the measure of all the fulness of God.

Augustine of Hippo
354 - 430

*'You have made us for yourself, and our hearts are restless till they rest in you.'
Augustine's most famous prayer could also be a comment on his own life.*

*Born at Tagaste in Algeria of a pagan father and a Christian mother, he was
brought up in the Christian faith. A brilliant student, he planned to become a lawyer
and studied rhetoric at the University of Carthage. There, puzzled by the problem of
evil, he rejected his childhood faith.*

*His mother Monica, however, continued to pray for him. While teaching in Milan,
Augustine came under the influence of Bishop Ambrose, and began to search for God.
The crisis came when, in the midst of a spiritual struggle, he heard a childish voice
saying, 'Tolle, lege' — 'Pick up and read'. He picked up the Bible, which he had formerly
despised, and the words he read drew him to God.*

*Within five years Augustine had become a bishop in his native North Africa. His
spiritual writings — the autobiographical 'Confessions' and the great theological work
'City of God' — have become classics of the faith for all time.*

The House of the Soul

O Lord, the house of my soul is narrow;
enlarge it, that you may enter in.
It is ruinous, O repair it!
It displeases your sight; I confess it, I know.
But who shall cleanse it, to whom shall I cry but to you?
Cleanse me from my secret faults, O Lord,
and spare your servant from strange sins.

Evening Prayer

Watch, dear Lord,
with those who wake, or watch, or weep tonight,
and give your angels charge over those who sleep.
Tend your sick ones, O Lord Christ,
rest your weary ones.
Bless your dying ones.
Soothe your suffering ones.
Pity your afflicted ones.
Shield your joyous ones.
And all for your love's sake,
Amen.

Prayer For God's Help

O God, from whom to be turned is to fall,
to whom to be turned is to rise,
and with whom to stand is to abide for ever;
grant us in all our duties your help,
in all our perplexities your guidance,
in all our dangers your protection,
and in all our sorrows your peace,
through Jesus Christ our Lord,
Amen.

Te Deum
FOURTH CENTURY

When Christians first met together for worship those who led the services prayed in their own words. But soon standard prayers were used — prayers which ensured that the important facts of the faith were brought to the congregation's mind. Some of these were based on biblical prayers, others arose out of the church's life.

By the fourth century, prayers used regularly in worship were being collected in written orders of service. The 'Te Deum', named after its opening words in Latin, dates from this period.

You are God and we praise you; you are the Lord and we acclaim you;
You are the eternal Father; all creation worships you.
To you all angels, all the powers of heaven,
Cherubim and seraphim sing in endless praise,
Holy holy holy Lord, God of power and might;
Heaven and earth are full of your glory.
The glorious company of apostles praise you;
The noble fellowship of prophets praise you;
The white-robed army of martyrs praise you.
Throughout the whole world the holy church acclaims you,
Father of majesty unbounded;
Your true and only Son worthy of all worship,
And the Holy Spirit advocate and guide.
You Christ are the King of glory,
The eternal Son of the Father.
When you became man to set us free
You did not abhor the virgin's womb.
You overcame the sting of death
And opened the kingdom of heaven to all believers.
You are seated at God's right hand in glory;
We believe that you will come and be our judge.
Come then Lord and help your people,
Bought with the price of your own blood;
And bring us with your saints
To glory everlasting.

Patrick of Ireland

390? - 461?

Ireland's patron saint was born somewhere on the west coast of England or Scotland — accounts of the place and date differ widely. At the age of sixteen he was captured by Irish pirates and kept as a slave for six years. While he tended his master's herd, he learnt to pray. 'In a single day,' he tells us in his autobiography, 'I said as many as a hundred prayers . . . I used to stay in the woods and on the mountain, and before the dawn I would be aroused to prayer, in snow and frost and rain . . . because then the spirit was fervent within.'

Eventually he escaped, found his family again and trained for the priesthood. He was sent as a missionary to Ireland by the pope, and set up a bishopric at Armagh. From here he travelled all over the country founding churches and monasteries. He was very conscious of his own lack of learning and anxious to promote education.

Many legends have grown up around him, but it is certainly true that Patrick was the major influence in converting Ireland to the Christian faith. His writings are the earliest British Christian literature. This prayer has been developed by a later writer from Patrick's original version.

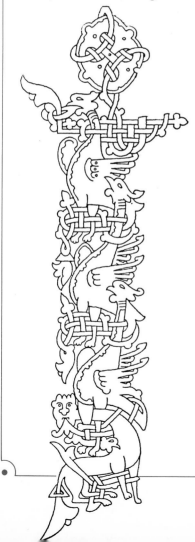

The Breastplate

I bind unto myself today
The power of God to hold and lead,
His eye to watch, his might to stay,
His ear to hearken to my need.
The wisdom of my God to teach,
His hand to guide, his shield to ward;
The word of God to give me speech,
His heavenly host to be my guard.

Christ be with me, Christ within me,
Christ behind me, Christ before me,
Christ beside me, Christ to win me,
Christ to comfort and restore me,
Christ beneath me, Christ above me,
Christ in quiet, Christ in danger,
Christ in mouth of friend or stranger.

I bind unto myself the name,
The strong name of the Trinity;
By invocation of the same,
The Three in One, the One in Three,
Of whom all nature hath creation;
Eternal Father, Spirit, Word,
Praise to the Lord of my salvation,
Salvation is of Christ the Lord.

Gelasian Sacramentary
SEVENTH OR EIGHTH CENTURY

In the early Western church, the book containing the order of service for the priest's guidance was known as a 'sacramentary'. Each sacramentary bore the name of a respected church leader who had composed the prayers or collected them together.

The 'Gelasian' sacramentary was associated with St Gelasius, pope from 492. However, the oldest manuscript of this book dates from the eighth century and was probably written by nuns at Chelles, near Paris.

The typical form of prayer in all sacramentaries is the 'collect', a short prayer said by the whole congregation. It usually begins by describing what God is like or recalling one of his acts in history, then asks for a blessing which links with this. Most of the prayers in the service books of the Reformation and later, including the 'Book of Common Prayer', come from the early Roman sacramentaries.

Eternal God
A PRAYER BASED ON AUGUSTINE

Eternal God,
the light of the minds that know you,
the life of the souls that love you,
the strength of the wills that serve you;
help us so to know you that we may truly love you,
so to love you that we may fully serve you,
whom to serve is perfect freedom.

An Evening Collect

Lighten our darkness, Lord, we pray; and in your mercy
defend us from all perils and dangers of this night; for the
love of your only Son, our Saviour Jesus Christ. Amen.

Celtic Prayers

The Irish were among the first people outside the Roman Empire to become Christians. In the fifth century they were cut off from the rest of the church by the barbarian invasions and developed their own distinctive forms of life and worship. Not until the eleventh and twelfth centuries were they again integrated with the rest of the church.

Their literature, like that of other Celtic languages, arose as the entertainment of an aristocratic social system. It was composed by paid writers supported by the court. Later, as that system broke down, a folk literature became popular, and many of the prayers come from this later period.

The Wish of Manchán of Liath

TENTH CENTURY

I wish, O Son of the living God, ancient eternal King, for a secret hut in the wilderness that it may be my dwelling.

A very blue shallow well to be beside it, a clear pool for washing away sins through the grace of the Holy Ghost.

A beautiful wood close by around it on every side, for the nurture of many-voiced birds, to shelter and hide it.

Facing the south for warmth, a little stream across its enclosure, a choice ground with abundant bounties which would be good for every plant.

A few sage disciples, I will tell their number, humble and obedient, to pray to the King.

Four threes, three fours, fit for every need, two sixes in the church both south and north.

Six couples in addition to me myself, praying through the long ages to the King who moves the sun.

A lovely church decked with linen, a dwelling for God of Heaven; then, bright candles over the holy white Scriptures.

One room to go to for the care of the body, without wantonness, without voluptuousness, without meditation of evil.

This is the housekeeping I would undertake, I would choose it without concealing: fragrant fresh leeks, hens, speckled salmon, bees.

My fill of clothing and of food from the King of good fame, and for me to be sitting for a while praying to God in every place.

25

Christ's Bounties
TADHG ÓG Ó HUIGINN, DIED 1448

O Son of God, do a miracle for me, and change my heart; thy having taken flesh to redeem me was more difficult than to transform my wickedness.

It is thou who, to help me, didst go to be scourged . . . thou, dear child of Mary, art the refined molten metal of our forge.

It is thou who makest the sun bright, together with the ice; it is thou who createdst the rivers and the salmon all along the river.

That the nut-tree should be flowering, O Christ, it is a rare craft; through thy skill too comes the kernel, thou fair ear of our wheat.

Though the children of Eve ill deserve the bird-flocks and the salmon, it was the Immortal One on the cross who made both salmon and birds.

It is he who makes the flower of the sloes grow through the surface of the blackthorn, and the nut-flower on other trees; beside this, what miracle is greater?

Anselm

1033-1109

Anselm was one of the most enlightened thinkers of his time; here, for instance, are his views on education:

'If you planted a tree in your garden, and bound it on all sides, so that it could not spread out its branches, what kind of a tree would it prove when in after years you gave it room to spread? Would it not be useless with its boughs all twisted and tangled? But that is how you treat your boys . . .!

These broad human sympathies expressed themselves in actions ranging from campaigning against the slave trade to rebuking a schoolboy for tying a bird's legs together.

The son of a spendthrift Lombard nobleman, Anselm left home after a quarrel with his father. He went to study under Lanfranc at Bec in Normandy, where he specialized in the study of Augustine and wrote important theological works. He went on to succeed Lanfranc in two positions — first as Abbot of Bec and then as Archbishop of Canterbury. Despite being exiled twice by King William Rufus, he was reconciled to the king and died in office at nearly eighty.

Desire For God

O Lord our God, grant us grace
to desire you with our whole heart,
that so desiring we may seek and find you,
and so finding you, may love you,
and loving you, may hate those sins
from which you have redeemed us.

A Call to Meditation

Come now, little man,
turn aside for a while from
your daily employment,
escape for a moment from
the tumult of your thoughts.
Put aside your weighty cares,
let your burdensome distractions wait,
free yourself awhile for God
and rest awhile in him.
Enter the inner chamber of your soul,
shut out everything except God
and that which can help you in seeking him,
and when you have shut the door, seek him.
Now, my whole heart, say to God,
'I seek your face,
Lord, it is your face I seek.'

Francis of Assisi

1181-1226

'The one saint everyone agrees in canonizing,' is one biographer's description of Francis, the son of a wealthy cloth merchant.

In a war between Assisi and Perugia, Francis was taken prisoner and became seriously ill. After a pilgrimage to Rome he returned to Assisi, and was praying in the ruined church of San Damiano, when he heard a voice saying, 'Go and repair my house.' Taking this literally, he sold some of his father's cloth and offered the money to the priest to rebuild the church.

Not surprisingly, this caused some conflict with his family! It came to a head when Francis stripped off all his clothes in the market-place and returned them to his father. From now on he regarded himself as 'married to Lady Poverty'.

With clothes given by the bishop, and money he had begged, Francis went off to rebuild San Damiano. He was soon joined by seven disciples, the first of what was to become the vast order of Franciscan friars. They lived in extreme poverty, preaching, labouring and serving the needy.

Many stories, true and legendary, have grown up around Francis: his preaching to the birds, his taming of a wolf, his receiving the marks of the wounds of Jesus. One of his more ambitious if less successful ventures was an effort to convert the Saracens. He died at only forty-five, worn out by poverty.

Canticle of the Sun

O most high, Almighty, good Lord God,
  to you belong praise, glory, honour,
  and all blessing!
Praised be my Lord God for all his
  creatures, especially for our brother
  the sun, who brings us the day and
  who brings us the light; fair is he
  and shines with a very great splendour;
  O Lord, he signifies you to us!
Praised be my Lord for our sister the moon,
  and for the stars, which he has set
  clear and lovely in heaven.
Praised be my Lord for our brother
  the wind, and for the air and clouds,
  calms and all weather by which you
  uphold life in all creatures.
Praised be my Lord for our sister water,
  who is very serviceable to us and
  humble and precious and clean.
Praised be my Lord for our brother fire,
  through whom you give us light in
  the darkness; and he is bright and
  pleasant and very mighty and strong.

Praised be my Lord for our mother the earth,
  who sustains us and keeps us and
  brings forth various fruits and flowers
  of many colours, and grass.
Praised be my Lord for all those who
  pardon one another for his love's sake,
  and who endure weakness and
  tribulation; blessed are they who shall
  peaceably endure, for you, O Most High,
  will give them a crown.
Praised be my Lord for our sister,
  the death of the body, from which
  no man escapes. Woe to him who dies
  in mortal sin!
Blessed are they who are found walking
  by your most holy will, for the
  second death shall have no power
  to do them harm.
Praise and bless the Lord,
  and give thanks to him
  and serve him with great humility.

You Are Holy

You are holy, Lord, the only God
and your deeds are wonderful.
You are strong, you are great.
You are the most High, you are almighty.
You, holy Father, are King of heaven and earth.
You are Three and One, Lord God, all good.
You are good, all good, supreme good,
Lord God, living and true.
You are love, you are wisdom.
You are humility, you are endurance.
You are rest, you are peace.
You are joy and gladness, you are justice and moderation.
You are all our riches, and you suffice for us.
You are beauty, you are gentleness.
You are our protector, you are our guardian and defender.
You are courage, you are our haven and our hope.
You are our faith, our great consolation.
You are our eternal life, great and wonderful Lord,
God almighty, merciful Saviour.

Instrument of Your Peace

Although this prayer cannot be traced further back than
the nineteenth century, it is always associated with Francis
of Assisi, and certainly reflects his spirit.

Lord, make me an instrument of your peace.
Where there is hatred, let me sow love,
Where there is injury, pardon,
Where there is doubt, faith,
Where there is despair, hope,
Where there is darkness, light,
Where there is sadness, joy.

O Divine Master, grant that I may not so much seek to be
consoled as to console,
not so much to be understood as to understand,
not so much to be loved, as to love;
for it is in giving that we receive,
it is in pardoning that we are pardoned,
it is in dying, that we awake to eternal life.

Richard of Chichester

1197-1253

In stained glass, Richard is often shown with a chalice at his feet. The story goes that he once dropped the chalice at communion but miraculously no wine was spilt!

Whatever the truth of this, Richard de Wych was certainly a saintly man. Born to a yeoman farmer at Droitwich, England, he was a studious boy but worked on a farm to help restore his family's fortunes. Later he studied canon law in Oxford and Europe. At Oxford he was so poor that he had to share a college gown and one warm tunic with two friends, and take it in turns to attend lectures!

His friend Edmund Rich, archbishop of Canterbury, appointed Richard chancellor of Oxford and then his personal assistant. They were exiled together for their political views. On his return to England Richard was made bishop of Chichester but the king refused to give him the material benefits that went with the post. Richard chose to live with the parish priest, growing figs and visiting his diocese on foot. He wore simple clothing, ate only vegetables and gave most of his money to the poor. He was described as 'a model diocesan bishop' and his grave was a place of pilgrimage until the sixteenth century.

Day By Day

Thanks be to thee,
Lord Jesus Christ,
for all the benefits
which thou hast won for us,
for all the pains and insults
which thou hast borne for us.
O most merciful Redeemer,
Friend and Brother,
may we know thee more clearly,
love thee more dearly,
and follow thee more nearly,
day by day.

Thomas Aquinas

1225-1274

Tall, well-built, tanned and balding, Thomas was known among his friends as 'the dumb Sicilian ox' because of his size and his usual silence at theological discussions. But his master at the University of Cologne predicted rightly that 'his lowing would soon be heard all over the world'.

Thomas resolved while a student at Naples that he would join the begging, or mendicant, order of Dominican friars. Even being kidnapped by his aristocratic family failed to stop him. He spent the rest of his life studying, writing and lecturing in theology in Paris and Italy. He had intense concentration, and was known to dictate to four secretaries at once. On one occasion he was sitting at the king's table in Paris, lost in thought, when he suddenly banged his fist on the table and cried, 'That's finished the heresy of the Manichees!' After apologies, a scribe was immediately sent for.

Thomas's writings formed the thinking of many generations of theologians. Yet on 6 December 1272 he had a revelation from God 'which made all I had written seem like so much straw'. After this he wrote no more.

A Steadfast Heart

Give me, O Lord, a steadfast heart,
which no unworthy affection may drag downwards;
give me an unconquered heart,
which no tribulation can wear out;
give me an upright heart,
which no unworthy purpose may tempt aside.
Bestow on me also, O Lord my God,
understanding to know you,
diligence to seek you,
wisdom to find you,
and a faithfulness that may finally embrace you,
through Jesus Christ our Lord, Amen.

Medieval Mystics

THIRTEENTH AND FOURTEENTH CENTURIES

'Sir, the pretending to extraordinary revelations and gifts of the Holy Ghost is a horrid thing, a very horrid thing,' said Bishop Butler to John Wesley in the eighteenth century. But many Christians throughout history would disagree with him. The apostle Paul himself hinted that he had received special revelations from God in an experience similar to that of many Christian mystics.

Mysticism emphasizes the individual's search for God through the discipline of deep prayer and meditation. This can open the door for God to communicate to the soul in an experience of great love, joy and peace; but on the way there may be a long struggle through spiritual dryness and depression. In the thirteenth and fourteenth centuries there was a great flowering of mystical experience all over Europe, and many classic works on the spiritual life were written.

Mechthild of Magdeburg

1210? -1280

Mechthild was the daughter of a noble family in Saxony, who left home in about 1230 to become a Beguine, a lay sister, not bound by vows, living in a religious community. Her visions of God were written down at the order of her confessor and published as 'The Light of Godhead'.

Lord, since you have taken from me all that I had from you, yet of your grace leave me the gift which every dog has by nature: that of being true to you in my distress, when I am deprived of all consolation. This I desire more fervently than your heavenly kingdom!

Johann Tauler

1300-1361

A disciple of the German mystical teacher Meister Eckhart, Tauler studied philosophy and theology in Cologne and Paris, and became a Dominican friar. His sermons to nuns on the nature and knowledge of God were widely read. In this prayer the myrrh represents suffering, and the incense worship.

May Jesus Christ, the king of glory, help us to make the right use of all the myrrh that God sends, and to offer to him the true incense of our hearts; for his name's sake, Amen.

Julian of Norwich

BORN ABOUT 1342

Little is known about Dame Julian except what she wrote in her autobiographical work 'Revelations of Divine Love'. As a young woman she had prayed for a greater understanding of Christ's sufferings and a physical illness to help her spiritually. At thirty both her prayers were answered. When on the point of death, she received the visions which are described in her book. The rest of her life was spent as a recluse, meditating on their meaning.

God, of your goodness, give me yourself; for you are sufficient for me. I cannot properly ask anything less, to be worthy of you. If I were to ask less, I should always be in want. In you alone do I have all.

Catherine of Siena
1347-1386

The twenty-fifth child of a Sienese dyer, Catherine Benincasa cut off her hair to make herself less attractive to suitors, wishing to devote her life to God. After punishing her by treating her as a servant, her parents finally allowed her to become a Dominican nun. Her fame as a spiritual authority spread so widely that she was even consulted on the negotiation of treaties. Although she never learnt to write, she dictated many letters and a book.

You, O eternal Trinity, are a deep sea, into which the more I enter the more I find, and the more I find the more I seek. The soul cannot be satiated in your abyss, for she continually hungers after you, the eternal Trinity, desiring to see you with the light of your light. As the hart desires the springs of living water, so my soul desires to leave the prison of this dark body and see you in truth.

O abyss, O eternal Godhead, O sea profound, what more could you give me than yourself? You are the fire that ever burns without being consumed; you consume in your heat all the soul's self-love; you are the fire which takes away cold; with your light you illuminate me so that I may know all your truth. Clothe me, clothe me with yourself, eternal truth, so that I may run this mortal life with true obedience, and with the light of your most holy faith.

Thomas à Kempis

1380-1471

The fourteenth century saw movements towards religious renewal all over Europe. Some Christians were rediscovering a direct experience of God through contemplation; others, such as the followers of Wycliffe in England, were translating the Bible into their own tongue and campaigning for greater involvement of the common people in the life of the church.

In Germany one such trend was represented by the Brethren of the Common Life, a community dedicated to promoting a deeper commitment to Christ. Thomas Hemerken from Kempen, near Cologne, better known as Thomas à Kempis, was educated at their school in Deventer. He was greatly influenced by their teachings. In 1399 he entered the Canons Regular at Zwolle as a lay brother living under a monastic rule, and in 1406 became a monk. He spent his time writing, preaching and copying manuscripts. But the best known product of his pen was 'The Imitation of Christ' — the most widely-read Christian book ever written.

For Discernment

Grant me, O Lord, to know what is worth knowing,
to love what is worth loving,
to praise what delights you most,
to value what is precious in your sight,
to hate what is offensive to you.
Do not let me judge by what I see,
nor pass sentence according to what I hear,
but to judge rightly between things that differ,
and above all to search out and to do what pleases you,
through Jesus Christ our Lord.

At the Start of a Day

Who can tell what a day may bring forth?
Cause me therefore, gracious God,
to live every day as if it were to be my
last, for I know not but that it may be
such. Cause me to live now as I shall wish
I had done when I come to die.
O grant that I may not die with any guilt
on my conscience, or any known sin
unrepented of, but that I may be found
in Christ, who is my only Saviour and
Redeemer.

Write Your Name

Write your blessed Name, O Lord,
upon my heart, there to remain so indelibly
engraved, that no prosperity, no adversity
shall ever move me from your love.
Be to me a strong tower of defence, a
comforter in tribulation, a deliverer in
distress, a very present help in trouble, and
a guide to heaven through the many
temptations and dangers of this life.

Submission to God's Will

O Lord, you know what is best for me. Let this or that be
done, as you please. Give what you will, how much you
will and when you will.

Desiderius Erasmus

1469?–1536

The leading scholar of his age, Erasmus wrote outspokenly against corruption in the Catholic church, but never joined the Protestant cause. Nevertheless his writings, which constantly advocated religious peace and freedom, were banned by two popes.

Educated by the Brethren of the Common Life, a lay Christian community, Erasmus rather reluctantly joined an order of Augustinian canons. But he soon left the monastic life to pursue his studies in the classics and the church fathers. His travels took him to Paris and then England. While there he met Thomas More and wrote the witty 'Encomium Morae' ('In Praise of Folly'), the title of which was a pun on his friend's name. After teaching Greek in Cambridge, Erasmus settled in Basle. There he continued to write and study, refusing many offers of political jobs in order to preserve his much-valued freedom.

To Be All to You

Sever me from myself that I may be grateful to you;
may I perish to myself that I may be safe in you;
may I die to myself that I may live in you;
may I wither to myself that I may blossom in you;
may I be emptied of myself that I may abound in you;
may I be nothing to myself that I may be all to you.

The Way, the Truth and the Life

O Lord Jesus Christ,
you have said that you are the way,
the truth, and the life.
Suffer us not to stray from you, who are the way,
nor to distrust you, who are the truth,
nor to rest in anything other than you,
who are the life.

Prayers Composed For St Paul's School, London

Hear our prayers, O Lord Jesus, the everlasting Wisdom of the Father. You give to us, in the days of our youth, aptness to learn. Add, we pray, the furtherance of your grace, so to learn knowledge and the liberal sciences that, by their help, we may attain to a fuller knowledge of you, whom to know is the height of blessedness; and by the example of your boyhood, may duly increase in age, wisdom and favour with God and man.

For Parents

O Lord God, whose will it is that, next to yourself, we should hold our parents in highest honour; it is not the least of our duties to beseech your goodness towards them. Preserve, I pray, my parents and home, in the love of your religion and in health of body, and mind. Grant that through me no sorrow may befall them; and finally, as they are kind to me, so may you be to them, O supreme Father of all.

Thomas More

1478-1535

The 1960s play and film 'A Man for All Seasons' had an unusual theme for its time: the moral dilemma of a sixteenth-century scholar torn between religious and political loyalties. Its success was a tribute to the lasting appeal of this man.

With his friend Erasmus, More was in the forefront of a remarkable revival of learning and ideas. More's book 'Utopia' expressed his vision for total political reform under the guise of an imaginary society. His brilliance as a speaker earned him a series of jobs in the government of King Henry VIII, and on the downfall of his former patron Cardinal Wolsey he became Chancellor of the Exchequer. But conflict arose over Henry's planned divorce. More would neither support this nor swear loyalty to Henry as head of the church in England. 'I am the King's good servant,' he said, 'but God's first.' This declaration led to his execution.

More was a man of wit, charm and charity. Even on the scaffold he showed his cheerful and determined character. 'Assist me up,' he told his executioner. 'Coming down, I can shift for myself.' The following prayer was written a week before his death.

Give Me, Good Lord

Glorious God, give me grace to amend my life, and to have an eye to my end without begrudging death, which to those who die in you, good Lord, is the gate of a wealthy life.

And give me, good Lord, a humble, lowly, quiet, peaceable, patient, charitable, kind, tender and pitiful mind, in all my works and all my words and all my thoughts, to have a taste of your holy, blessed Spirit.

Give me, good Lord, a full faith, a firm hope, and a fervent charity, a love of you incomparably above the love of myself.

Give me, good Lord, a longing to be with you, not to avoid the calamities of this world, nor so much to attain the joys of heaven, as simply for love of you.

And give me, good Lord, your love and favour, which my love of you, however great it might be, could not deserve were it not for your great goodness.

These things, good Lord, that I pray for, give me your grace to labour for.

Prayers of the Reformers

SIXTEENTH CENTURY

Undoubtedly the most dramatic moment of the Reformation was when Martin Luther nailed his ninety-five theses, or points for discussion, on the door of the cathedral at Wittenberg. But his action was both the climax of a long process of preparation, and the start of a century or more of intense argument, thought, prayer and writing.

All over Europe others, like Luther, sought to restore the church to the basics of faith by stripping away the additions which had gradually obscured the message of Jesus. Most found that they could not achieve this without breaking away from the Catholic church of their time. They became, often reluctantly, the founders of a new movement — the Protestant church.

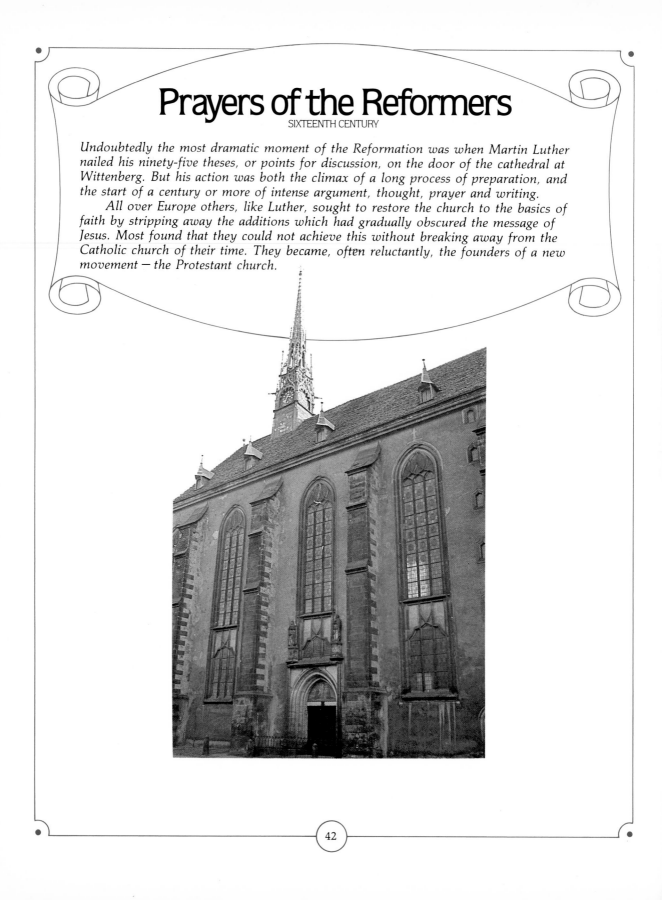

Martin Luther
1483-1546

A miner's son from Saxony, Luther became a monk in fulfilment of a vow he had made during a thunderstorm. Having studied philosophy he became a lecturer at the newly-founded Wittenberg University, and was soon a Doctor of Theology and professor of Scripture. Tormented by doubts about his standing before God, in about 1512 he experienced an overwhelming conviction that it was by faith in Christ alone he could be saved. From now on he fought everything in the church that contradicted this.

His campaign earned him a trial for heresy, during which he spoke the famous words, 'Here I stand; I can do no other.' This was followed by excommunication and imprisonment for his own safety. But his fame quickly spread and he gained much support. He wrote prolifically and his translation of the Bible into popular language contributed greatly to the development of modern German.

The Empty Vessel

Behold, Lord, an empty vessel that needs to be filled. My Lord, fill it. I am weak in the faith; strengthen me. I am cold in love; warm me and make me fervent, that my love may go out to my neighbour. I do not have a strong and firm faith; at times I doubt and am unable to trust you altogether. O Lord, help me. Strengthen my faith and trust in you. In you I have sealed the treasure of all I have. I am poor; you are rich and came to be merciful to the poor. I am a sinner; you are upright. With me, there is an abundance of sin; in you is the fullness of righteousness. Therefore I will remain with you, of whom I can receive, but to whom I may not give.

Miles Coverdale
1488-1568

An Augustinian monk who became a supporter of the Reformation, Coverdale made his great contribution by translating the Bible into the English of his day. During the reign of Mary Tudor, he was exiled to Geneva where he translated many works of the European reformers.

When Persecuted

O God, give us patience when the wicked hurt us. O how impatient and angry we are when we think ourselves unjustly slandered, reviled and hurt! Christ suffers strokes upon his cheek, the innocent for the guilty; yet we may not abide one rough word for his sake. O Lord, grant us virtue and patience, power and strength, that we may take all adversity with good will, and with a gentle mind overcome it. And if necessity and your honour require us to speak, grant that we may do so with meekness and patience, that the truth and your glory may be defended, and our patience and steadfast continuance perceived.

Thomas Cranmer

1489-1556

Archbishop of Canterbury in the reign of King Henry VIII, Cranmer was a man of immense learning: his personal library was larger than that of Cambridge University and he could read Latin, Greek, Hebrew, French, Italian and German. In 1538 he ordered that an English translation of the Bible should be placed in every church and read aloud regularly. But his greatest achievement was to compile the 'Book of Common Prayer', an English order of worship published in 1549 to replace the complicated medieval Latin services. Using both old and new prayers, he changed the church's worship from a mysterious ceremony in which the congregation were merely onlookers to an act of worship in which all could paritipate. He was martyred under Mary Tudor but his work, in revised forms, continues to be used four hundred years later.

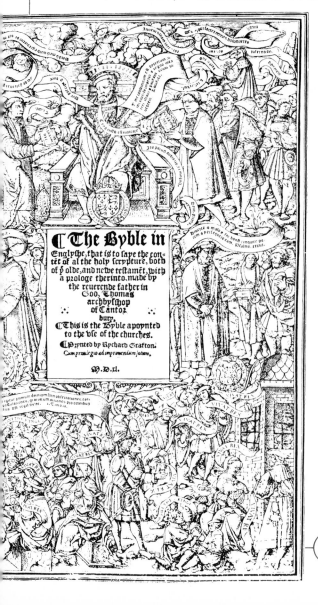

Collect For Advent

Almighty God,
give us grace to cast away the works of darkness
and put on the armour of light,
now in the time of this mortal life,
in which your Son Jesus Christ came to us
in great humility;
so that on the last day,
when he shall come again in glorious majesty
to judge both the living and the dead,
we may rise to the life immortal,
through him who is alive and reigns with you
and the Holy Spirit,
now and ever,
Amen.

Collect For Lent

Almighty and everlasting God,
you hate nothing that you have made,
and forgive the sins of all those who are penitent.
Create and make in us new and contrite hearts,
that, lamenting our sins
and acknowledging our wretchedness,
we may receive from you, the God of all mercy,
perfect forgiveness and peace;
through Jesus Christ our Lord,
Amen.

Philip Melanchthon
1497-1560

Philip Scwarzerd was nicknamed 'Melanchthon' (the Greek equivalent of his surname) because of his interest in Greek studies. A friend and fellow-lecturer of Luther's, he published Luther's early writings and, using the name 'Didymus Faventinus', wrote in Luther's defence.

Prayer For Unity

To you, O Son of God, Lord Jesus Christ, as you pray to
the eternal Father, we pray, make us one in him. Lighten
our personal distress and that of our society. Receive us
into the fellowship of those who believe. Turn our hearts,
O Christ, to everlasting truth and healing harmony.

John Calvin

1509-1564

Born in Picardy, France, Calvin gave up his intention to become a priest after a vision calling him to restore the church to its original purity. During persecution, he fled to Basle and started to write his great work, the 'Institutes'. Settling in Geneva, he embarked on a campaign of moral reform designed to make the city a centre of Christian living. By his death he had total political and religious power in Geneva. The main emphasis in his thinking was on the sinfulness of man, the power of God and the importance of the Bible.

Before Reading Scripture

O Lord, heavenly Father, in whom is the fullness of light
and wisdom, enlighten our minds by your Holy Spirit,
and give us grace to receive your Word with reverence
and humility, without which no one can understand your
truth. For Christ's sake, Amen.

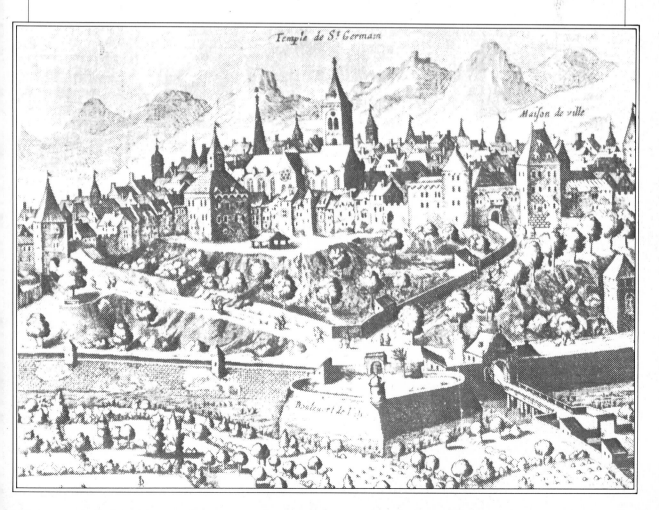

John Knox

1513-1572

The main creator of the Scottish prayer book, Knox was a notary and private tutor before becoming a famous preacher. He was chaplain to Edward VI of England and later came into violent conflict with Mary, Queen of Scots, whom he regarded as a 'scarlet woman' for her worldly life and her Catholic faith.

Blessing At a Wedding

The Lord sanctify and bless you,
the Lord pour the riches of his grace upon you,
that you may please him
and live together in holy love
to your lives' end.
So be it.

Ignatius Loyola

1491-1556

The youngest of eleven children of a Basque nobleman, Ignatius was brought up to be a soldier. Convalescing from a bad leg wound received in battle, he asked for some knightly romances to read. Instead he was given a life of Christ and a collection of the stories of the saints. It was the beginning of a new life.

Ignatius spent a year in prayer and penance, and then began to write his great work, the 'Spiritual Exercises'. After a time of imprisonment as a heretic, he left Spain for Paris to study Latin and philosophy, gaining his master's degree at forty-three. In Paris he gathered six disciples, who became the core of a new movement — the Company of Jesus, or Jesuits. Their aim was to provide a spiritual and intellectual foundation for Catholic renewal, in response to the growth of Protestantism. Ignatius was their general, modelling his leadership on military-style authority and demanding total obedience. By the time of his death there were 1,000 Jesuits involved in education, foreign missions and social service.

A leader of iron will, Ignatius was also a man of fervent spirituality. As a student in Paris he once tried to conjugate the Latin verb 'amare' (to love) but was only able to repeat over and over again, 'I love God . . . I am loved by God.'

For Dedication to God

Teach us, Lord,
to serve you as you deserve,
to give and not to count the cost,
to fight and not to heed the wounds,
to toil and not to seek for rest,
to labour and not to ask for any reward
save that of knowing that we do your will.

A Prayer of Surrender

Take, Lord, all my liberty,
my memory, my understanding,
and my whole will.
You have given me all that I have,
all that I am,
and I surrender all to your divine will,
that you dispose of me.
Give me only your love and your grace.
With this I am rich enough,
and I have no more to ask.

Sarum Primer Prayer
1514?

The title of this prayer comes from a book published in the English medieval cathedral town of Salisbury (known by its Latin name of Sarum) in 1558. But it must have been written at an earlier date for it is found in a 1514 'book of hours' or private service book, in Clare College, Cambridge. It seems to have been used as a private prayer said before reading the 'offices', or set prayers, for the day. In 1908 it was published as a hymn, set to music by Sir Walford Davies, and has since become very popular especially in British schools.

God be in my head
and in my understanding;
God be in my eyes
and in my looking;
God be in my mouth
and in my speaking;
God be in my heart
and in my thinking;
God be at my end
and at my departing.

Teresa of Avila

1515-1582

As a small child, Teresa played with her brother at 'hermitages', pretending to be religious recluses; once they ran away to 'die as martyrs in Morocco'. Her teenage years were occupied with fashions and romantic reading, but during an illness she read the works of Jerome and decided to become a nun. Despite her aristocratic father's opposition she entered a convent at twenty.

Convents at this time were very easy-going, and Teresa lived a pleasurable life. But in 1555 she had a mystical experience of God which transformed her life. After being ridiculed for her visions, she founded a new convent with a stricter rule at her birthplace of Avila in Spain. This was the beginning of a new order, the 'barefoot' Carmelites.

Teresa's nuns wore coarse brown habits and sandals, ate no meat and spent their days doing manual work which Teresa herself shared. She was very careful in selecting candidates: 'God preserve us from stupid nuns!' was her cry. Her books combine a very practical approach to the religious life with a deep love of God. She died on her way back from founding her sixteenth convent.

Silly Devotions

From silly devotions
and from sour-faced saints,
good Lord, deliver us.

Teresa's Bookmark

Let nothing disturb you;
let nothing dismay you;
all things pass:
God never changes.
Patience attains
all it strives for.
He who has God
finds he lacks nothing:
God alone suffices.

Christ's Body

Christ has no body now on earth but yours;
yours are the only hands with which he can do his work,
yours are the only feet with which he can go about
the world,
yours are the only eyes through which his compassion
can shine forth upon a troubled world.
Christ has no body now on earth but yours.

John Donne

1571-1631

'A second St Augustine' was how Isaac Walton, his first biographer, described Donne. The likeness to Augustine included a weakness for women — Donne's 'profane' poems describe a succession of mistresses — and a long struggle to find his faith.

For a time Donne was greatly attracted to Roman Catholicism, but eventually he left a somewhat chequered career in law to be ordained into the Church of England. Only a few years after his ordination he was appointed Dean of St Paul's Cathedral in London, where his statue can still be seen. His sermons, like his poems, won him fame for their powerful imagery and striking language. Their eloquence flows from a passionate faith which involved both his intellect and his emotions.

A Vision of Heaven

Bring us, O Lord God, at the last awakening into the house and gate of heaven, to enter into that gate and dwell in that house, where there shall be no darkness nor dazzling, but one equal light; no noise nor silence, but one equal music; no fears nor hopes, but an equal possession; no ends nor beginnings, but one equal eternity, in the habitations of thy majesty and thy glory, world without end.

Reliance On God

O Lord,
never suffer us to think
that we can stand by ourselves,
and not need thee.

Prayer of an Ageing Woman

ANONYMOUS

Usually attributed to a seventeenth-century nun, this prayer is in fact of unknown origin — but its sentiments are only too familiar!

Lord, you know better than I know myself that I am growing older, and will some day be old. Keep me from getting talkative, and particularly from the fatal habit of thinking that I must say something on every subject and on every occasion.

Release me from craving to straighten out everybody's affairs. Make me thoughtful but not moody; helpful but not bossy. With my vast store of wisdom it seems a pity not to use it all, but you know, Lord, that I want a few friends at the end. Keep my mind from the recital of endless details — give me wings to come to the point.

I ask for grace enough to listen to the tales of others' pains. But seal my lips on my own aches and pains — they are increasing, and my love of rehearsing them is becoming sweeter as the years go by. Help me to endure them with patience.

I dare not ask for improved memory, but for a growing humility and a lessening cocksureness when my memory seems to clash with the memories of others. Teach me the glorious lesson that occasionally it is possible that I may be mistaken.

Keep me reasonably sweet. I do not want to be a saint — some of them are so hard to live with — but a sour old woman is one of the crowning works of the devil.

Give me the ability to see good things in unexpected places, and talents in unexpected people. And give me, O Lord, the grace to tell them so.

New England Sampler
SIXTEENTH OR SEVENTEENTH CENTURY

Before printed pattern books came into use in 1523, stitches for embroidery were demonstrated on linen panels known as 'samplers'. In the seventeenth century the sampler became a school exercise; every young girl was expected to sew at least one sampler to show her skill in feminine 'accomplishments'. The sampler usually included a domestic scene or a picture of a house with people around it. Central to the design would be a prayer, a text from the Bible, or a pious proverb, so that when the sampler was framed and hung on the wall it would remind its creator and her family of their religious duties.

God bless all those that I love;
God bless all those that love me;
God bless all those that love those that I love
and all those that love those that love me.

Blaise Pascal
1623-1662

A very precocious boy, Pascal was educated privately in his home town of Clermont-Ferrand, France. At seventeen he devised one of the first calculating machines, based on a mechanism of rotating discs. Later he discovered Pascal's Law, a principle of water pressure which forms the basis for modern hydraulics.

On 23 January 1654 he had a deep spiritual experience in which he discovered 'the God of Abraham, the God of Isaac, the God of Jacob, and not of philosophers and men of science'. He wrote down his feelings at the time and carried the paper around with him for the rest of his life, sewn into the lining of his coat.

His unfinished writings on faith were collected together and published after his death as 'Pensées'. In this meditative work he stresses the emotional dimension of faith and the fact that God cannot be reached by reason: 'the heart has its reasons of which reason knows nothing'.

Conform My Will

O Lord, let me not henceforth desire health or life except to spend them for you, with you and in you. You alone know what is good for me; do therefore what seems best to you. Give to me or take from me; conform my will to yours; and grant that with humble and perfect submission and in holy confidence I may receive the orders of your eternal providence, and may equally adore all that comes to me from you.

Folk Prayers
TRADITIONAL

From the Celtic church of the Dark Ages to the Negro slaves in America, ordinary people have always composed prayers which were worth handing down to successive generations. Usually short and direct but often with poetic charm and wry humour, such prayers reveal a simple and firmly-rooted faith in a God who is concerned with the practical, everyday details of life.

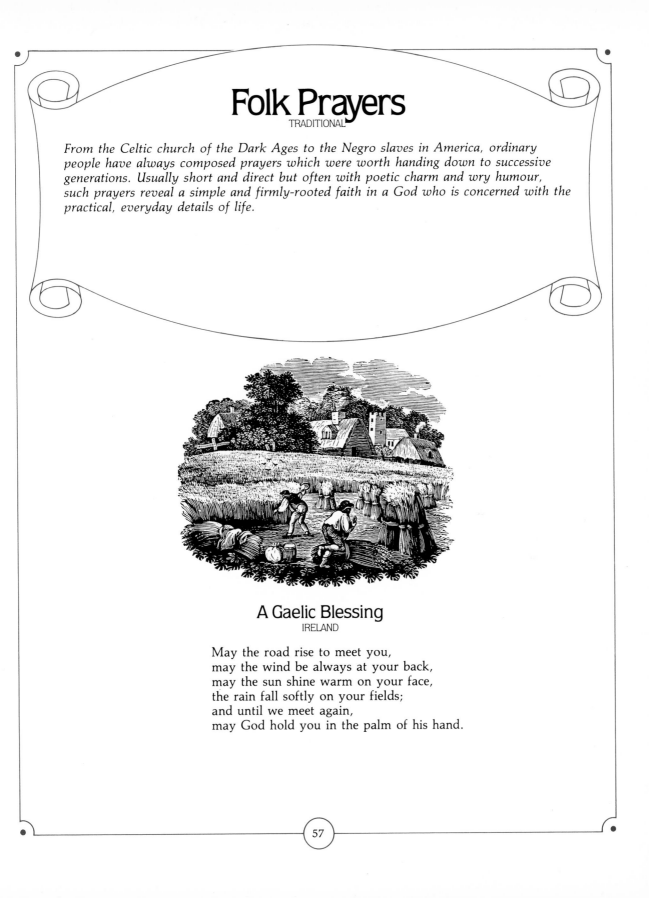

A Gaelic Blessing
IRELAND

May the road rise to meet you,
may the wind be always at your back,
may the sun shine warm on your face,
the rain fall softly on your fields;
and until we meet again,
may God hold you in the palm of his hand.

The Breton Fisherman's Prayer
FRANCE

Dear God, be good to me. The sea is so wide, and my
boat is so small.

Prayer For the Animals
RUSSIA

Hear our humble prayer, O God, for our friends the
animals. We entreat for them all your mercy and pity, and
for those who deal with them we ask a heart of
compassion, gentle hands and kindly words. Make us
ourselves to be true friends to animals and so to share the
blessing of the merciful. For the sake of your Son, the
tender-hearted Jesus Christ our Lord.

Negro Prayers
AMERICA

O Lord, help me to understand that you ain't going to let nothing come my way that you and me together can't handle.

Prayer of a negro boy running a race:
Lord, you pick 'em up and I'll put 'em down, you pick 'em up and I'll put 'em down . . .

A Child's Prayer
ENGLAND

Make me, dear Lord, polite and kind
To everyone, I pray;
And may I ask you how you find
Yourself, dear Lord, today?

Jonathan Edwards

1703-1758

'On January 12th 1723', writes Edwards, 'I made a solemn dedication of myself to God and wrote it down; giving up myself and all that I had to God; to be for the future in no respect my own.' This was the climax of two years of intense searching for God. The fruit of Edward's dedication is described in his 'Faithful Narrative of the Surprising Work of God', an account of how his preaching in Northampton, Massachusetts, brought thousands to a new faith in Christ. Through his preaching and spiritual writings he became one of the most important figures in the history of the American church.

Edwards' views and methods, however, were not universally popular; and in 1750, after a long conflict, he was dismissed by his congregation. He continued to preach and write, particularly urging Christians to pray for new spiritual life in the nation. In 1758 he was elected president of the college which was to become Princeton University, but died of smallpox only two months after his appointment.

Devotion to God's Work

FROM THE FUNERAL SERVICE FOR MISSIONARY DAVID BRAINERD

Oh that the things which were seen and heard in this extraordinary person; his holiness, heavenliness, labour and self-denial in life; his so remarkably devoting himself and his all, in heart and practice, to the glory of God; and the wonderful frame of mind manifested, in so steadfast a manner, under the expectation of death, and under the pains and agonies which brought it on; may excite in us all, both ministers and people, a due sense of the greatness of the work which we have to do in the world, of the excellency and amiableness of thorough religion in experience and practice, of the blessedness of the end of those whose death finishes such a life, and of the infinite value of their eternal reward . . . and effectually stir us up to constant endeavours that, in the way of such a holy life, we may at last come to as blessed an end! Amen.

John Wesley

1703-1791

On 24 May 1738 an earnest, pious but discontented young man listened to a reading from Luther's 'Preface to Romans' at a religious meeting in Aldersgate, London. Suddenly he felt his heart 'strangely warmed' and a new, overwhelming sense of God's love possessed him.

Wesley, the fifteenth son of a Lincolnshire clergyman, was already active in promoting Christianity. But his experience in Aldersgate gave his faith a new confidence and vigour. The rest of his life was dedicated to spreading the gospel to the thousands who were untouched by the church.

He travelled an average of 8,000 miles a year on horseback to preach to huge crowds in the open air: 'I regard the whole world as my parish,' he said. This revolutionary approach to evangelism could not be contained within the Anglican church of his time. So a new denomination was born: the Methodists, nicknamed from the methodical study of spiritual matters the 'Holy Club' had started. Regular prayer, alone and in small groups, was the life-blood of the Methodist church. 'Pray without ceasing,' Wesley wrote on the fly-leaf of his private diary, and he dedicated an hour each morning and evening to prayer.

A Plea For Forgiveness

Forgive them all, O Lord:
our sins of omission and our sins of commission;
the sins of our youth and the sins of our riper years;
the sins of our souls and the sins of our bodies;
our secret and our more open sins;
our sins of ignorance and surprise,
and our more deliberate and presumptuous sin;
the sins we have done to please ourselves
and the sins we have done to please others;
the sins we know and remember,
and the sins we have forgotten;
the sins we have striven to hide from others
and the sins by which we have made others offend;
forgive them, O Lord, forgive them all for his sake,
who died for our sins and rose for our justification,
and now stands at thy right hand to make intercession
for us,
Jesus Christ our Lord.

Meditation on the Cross

O Jesus, poor and abject, unknown and despised, have mercy upon me, and let me not be ashamed to follow thee.

O Jesus, hated, calumniated, and persecuted, have mercy upon me, and make me content to be as my master.

O Jesus, blasphemed, accused, and wrongfully condemned, have mercy upon me, and teach me to endure the contradiction of sinners.

O Jesus, clothed with a habit of reproach and shame, have mercy upon me, and let me not seek my own glory.

O Jesus, insulted, mocked, and spit upon, have mercy upon me, and let me not faint in the fiery trial.

O Jesus, crowned with thorns and hailed in derision;

O Jesus, burdened with our sins and the curses of the people;

O Jesus, affronted, outraged, buffeted, overwhelmed with injuries, griefs and humiliations;

O Jesus, hanging on the accursed tree, bowing the head, giving up the ghost, have mercy upon me, and conform my whole soul to to thy holy, humble, suffering Spirit.

This Transitory Life

Fix thou our steps, O Lord, that we stagger not at the uneven motions of the world, but steadily go on to our glorious home; neither censuring our journey by the weather we meet with, nor turning out of the way for anything that befalls us.

The winds are often rough, and our own weight presses us downwards. Reach forth, O Lord, thy hand, thy saving hand, and speedily deliver us.

Teach us, O Lord, to use this transitory life as pilgrims returning to their beloved home; that we may take what our journey requires, and not think of settling in a foreign country.

Prayers of Missionaries

EIGHTEENTH—TWENTIETH CENTURIES

In the eighteenth and nineteenth centuries, religious revivals such as that begun by Wesley triggered off a new interest in bringing the good news of Jesus to people all over the world. Many missionary societies were founded; most had a special interest in one particular part of the world.

Those who offered themselves for missionary service faced hardship, loneliness and often danger. Some of them became famous through their diaries and other writings, and inspired many others to follow them in dedicating their lives to God's service.

Henry Martyn
1781-1812

A brilliant linguist, Martyn was the first Englishman to offer himself for service with the newly-formed Church Missionary Society, which, however, refused him. Instead he went to India as a chaplain with the East India Company, and spent most of his life translating the New Testament and the 'Book of Common Prayer' into Hindustani. Advised to take a sea voyage for his health, he travelled to Persia and there translated the New Testament into Arabic and Persian. He died in Armenia on his way home.

Blind and Helpless

Lord, I am blind and helpless,
stupid and ignorant.
Cause me to hear;
cause me to know;
teach me to do;
lead me.

Prayer of Dedication
ON FINISHING HIS PERSIAN TRANSLATION
OF THE NEW TESTAMENT

Now may the Spirit,
who gave the Word,
and called me, I trust,
to be an interpreter of it,
graciously and powerfully
apply it to the hearts of sinners.

Temple Gairdner

1873-1928

Temple Gairdner was sent by the Church Missionary Society to Cairo in 1898. Already experienced in working with students in the University of Oxford, his aim was to spread the Christian faith amongst the students and educated classes of Egypt. He taught colloquial Arabic to missionaries and Egyptian teachers, wrote textbooks on phonetics, translated hymns, poems and plays, started an Arabic-English Christian magazine, and collected over 300 traditional local tunes for use in worship. He loved music, poetry and nature and enjoyed all of life intensely.

His First Spoken Prayer

O God,
you know that I do not want anything else
but to serve you and men, always, all my life.

A 'Lost Life'

Lord, I am willing to appear to the world and to all to have lost my life, if only I may have made it good in your sight.

Prayer Before His Marriage

That I may come near to her,
draw me nearer to you than to her;
that I may know her,
make me to know you more than her;
that I may love her
with the love of a perfectly whole heart,
cause me to love you more than her and most of all.

Amy Carmichael
1868-1951

Amy Carmichael's account of her work, 'Things as they are', removed the glamour from the idea of missionary life but at the same time led many to follow her example. Forced to leave her work in Japan because of ill-health, she went to South India and there founded the Dohnavur Fellowship to rescue children from the degradation of Hindu temple service. In spite of crippling arthritis she wrote many books of devotions and poems based on her experiences.

Think Through Me

Holy Spirit
think through me
till your ideas
are my ideas.

It Is Not Far

It is not far to go
for you are near.
It is not far to go,
for you are here.
And not by travelling, Lord,
men come to you,
but by the way of love,
and we love you.

John Henry Newman

1801-1890

While vicar of the university church in Oxford, Newman became leader of the Oxford Movement, a group of clergy and laity who responded to the growing attacks on Christianity in their time by seeking to help the Church of England return to its historic roots. In particular, they advocated a more traditional style of worship, closer to that of the Roman Catholic church.

Newman preached and wrote vigorously in support of these beliefs and encountered much opposition. Eventually he saw that he would not find what he sought in the Anglican church. In 1845 he was received into the Roman Catholic church; the following year he was ordained a priest, and by 1879 he had been made a cardinal.

In 1864 the author Charles Kingsley wrote rather unfairly of Newman that he 'did not consider truth a necessary virtue'. This attack led Newman to publish his 'Apologia pro Vita Sua', a remarkable autobiography defending his views and actions.

O Lord, Support Us
USED BY NEWMAN BUT PROBABLY OF SIXTEENTH-CENTURY ORIGIN

O Lord, support us all the day long, until the shadows lengthen and the evening comes, and the busy world is hushed, and the fever of life is over, and our work is done. Then, Lord, in your mercy grant us a safe lodging, and a holy rest, and peace at the last; through Jesus Christ our Lord.

The Fragrance of Christ

Help me to spread your fragrance everywhere I go — let me preach you without preaching, not by words but by my example — by the catching force, the sympathetic influence of what I do, the evident fullness of the love my heart bears to you.

Lord Shaftesbury
1801-1885

On a rainy day in 1885 a funeral procession wound its way to Westminster Abbey. In it were people from all walks of life: representatives of religious societies and charities, flower sellers, street urchins, aristocrats, chimney sweeps, statesmen, clergymen. This motley crowd represented the wide range of interests of Anthony Ashley Cooper, the Earl of Shaftesbury, whose coffin they followed.

Through legislation and campaigning Shaftesbury sought to defend the rights of women and children who worked in the mines, small boys who climbed chimneys to clean them, the mentally ill, the milliners and dressmakers who worked in sweatshops. He promoted industrial training, 'ragged' schools for the poor, and the work of organizations involved in urban and overseas evangelism and social work. His life was governed by the principle he had written down in his twenty-seventh year: 'The first principle God's honour, the second man's happiness, the means prayer and unremitting diligence.'

Father of the Forsaken

O God, the father of the forsaken, the help of the weak, the supplier of the needy; you teach us that love towards the race of man is the bond of perfectness, and the imitation of your blessed self. Open and touch our hearts that we may see and do, both for this world and that which is to come, the things that belong to our peace. Strengthen us in the work which we have undertaken; give us wisdom, perseverance, faith, and zeal, and in your own time and according to your pleasure prosper the issue; for the love of your Son Jesus Christ.

Abraham Lincoln

1809 -1865

The hero of American politics was also the embodiment of American ideals: a 'self-made man'. Of humble origins, he became by his own efforts a lawyer, practising in Illinois in the 1830s and '40s. After a term in Congress as a Democrat, he became a Republican in 1856 and engaged in a series of public debates with Senator Stephen A. Douglas in an attempt to gain Douglas's seat in the Senate. The attempt failed, but the debates had made Lincoln's name known and in 1860 he was elected president.

Almost immediately the country was plunged into the Civil War, and in 1863 he proclaimed the slaves in the Southern states free as a war measure. He was hailed from then on as a champion of liberty and his famous speech at Gettysburg became the charter of American freedom. But only days after the victory of the Union in 1865 he was assassinated by a gunman during a theatre visit.

For a Nation At War

Grant, O merciful God, that with malice toward none,
with charity to all, with firmness in the right as thou
givest us to see the right, we may strive to finish the work
we are in; to bind up the nation's wounds; to care for him
who shall have borne the battle and for his widow and his
orphan; to do all which may achieve and cherish a just
and lasting peace among ourselves and with all nations.

Right and Might

Lord, give us faith that right makes might.

Søren Kierkegaard
1813-1855

'Christ came in through locked doors' was how Kierkegaard described his conversion. The seventh child of a wealthy father, he lived in Copenhagen nearly all his life, first studying theology and then writing. He was a familiar figure in the theatres and cafés of the city, well known for his brilliance and wit. But underneath the superficial joviality was a persistent melancholy, intensified in 1841 by his broken engagement.

His numerous writings cover aesthetics, philosophy, religion; many of them were written under pseudonyms so he could state his views more freely. He was severely criticized for his attacks on bourgeois religiosity. 'My very humble work,' he wrote, 'is to make people aware . . . to make room that God may come.'

The Thought of God

Father in heaven, when the thought of you wakes in our
hearts, let it not wake like a frightened bird that flies
about in dismay, but like a child waking from its sleep
with a heavenly smile.

Prayer For a Meeting

Holy Spirit, you make alive;
bless also this our gathering,
the speaker and the hearer;
fresh from the heart it shall come,
by your aid,
let it also go to the heart.

Faith

Teach me,
O God,
not to torture myself,
not to make a martyr out of myself
through stifling reflection,
but rather teach me to breathe deeply in faith.

Florence Nightingale

1820-1910

'She taught nurses to be ladies and brought ladies out of the bondage of idleness to be nurses' commented one biographer. The daughter of a country gentleman, Florence rebelled against an enforced life of leisure. At this time nursing was a barely respectable occupation in England, so she travelled abroad and spent eleven years visiting hospitals in Europe run by Protestant and Catholic sisterhoods. Deeply impressed by their commitment and devotion, she returned in 1853 to become superintendent of a London hospital for 'invalid gentlewomen'.

A year later the Crimean War broke out. Reading about the contrast between the care of the wounded French soldiers and the neglect of the English ones, Florence offered her services as superintendent of the female nurses. Out of incredibly sordid conditions she created order. To do so she worked twenty hours a day.

In 1856 fever forced her to come home — to a hero's welcome. Among the honours shown her was the gift of a brooch designed by Prince Albert, a diamond bracelet from the Sultan of Turkey, a poem written about her by the American poet Longfellow, medals from England, France, Germany and Norway, and the freedom of the City of London. Although an invalid, she went on working to the end of her life. She established a school for nurses in London and took a keen interest in medical work in India.

Where Are You Leading?

Oh God, you put into my heart this great desire to devote myself to the sick and sorrowful; I offer it to you. Do with it what is for your service.

Oh my Creator, are you leading every man of us to perfection? Or is this only a metaphysical idea for which there is no evidence? Is man only a constant repetition of himself? You know that through all these twenty horrible years I have been supported by the belief (I think I must believe it still or I am sure I could not work) that I was working with you who were bringing every one of us, even our poor nurses, to perfection. O Lord, even now I am trying to snatch the management of your world from your hands. Too little have I looked for something higher and better than my own work — the work of supreme Wisdom, which uses us whether we know it or not.

Fyodor Dostoevsky
1821-1881

Dostoevsky began his career as a student at a military engineering college in St Petersburg, but soon turned to writing. In 1849 he was arrested for revolutionary activities, condemned to death but reprieved and sent to Siberia for ten years. It was during this period that he developed his great love for the common people.

He then became involved in journalism, publishing a democratic review with his brother. Unhappily married for seven years, on the death of his first wife he married his secretary. Both his political experiences and his personal sufferings through his first marriage, his epilepsy and his financial troubles are reflected in his great novels. In these, as in the writings of Kierkegaard, there is a strong emphasis on salvation through suffering. The established church is portrayed as a tyrant, and the central characters are marked by intense emotion and universal compassion.

Love of Life
ADAPTED FROM A PASSAGE IN 'THE BROTHERS KARAMAZOV'

Lord, may we love all your creation, all the earth and every grain of sand in it. May we love every leaf, every ray of your light.

May we love the animals: you have given them the rudiments of thought and joy untroubled. Let us not trouble it; let us not harass them, let us not deprive them of their happiness, let us not work against your intent.

For we acknowledge unto you that all is like an ocean, all is flowing and blending, and that to withhold any measure of love from anything in your universe is to withhold that same measure from you.

Christina Rossetti

1830 -1894

Christina Rossetti's first verses were written to her mother on her birthday in 1842, and during the same year her Italian grandfather published a collection of her work privately. At nineteen she was writing for a journal published by friends of her brother, the artist Dante Gabriel Rossetti. Before long her poetry was widely known and she became one of the most popular poets of her time.

Her work included love poetry and poems for children, but a large part of her output was devotional poetry and prose. It was her deep and passionate Christian faith that led her to break off one engagement and refuse another offer of marriage (even though she loved the second man deeply) because neither of the men shared her faith. She 'took the veil in every way except in outward act' according to one biographer. Living with her widowed mother, she spent her time doing charitable works and later, suffering from the rare Graves' Disease, became virtually a recluse.

In Weariness

O Lord, Jesus Christ,
who art as the shadow of a great rock in a weary land,
who beholdest thy weak creatures
weary of labour, weary of pleasure,
weary of hope deferred, weary of self;
in thine abundant compassion,
and fellow feeling with us,
and unutterable tenderness,
bring us, we pray thee,
unto thy rest.

To the Holy Spirit

As the wind is thy symbol
so forward our goings.
As the dove
so launch us heavenwards.
As water
so purify our spirits.
As a cloud
so abate our temptations.
As dew
so revive our languor.
As fire
so purge out our dross.

Eugène Bersier
1831-1889

After theological studies in his native Switzerland and then in Germany, Bersier ministered in Paris to a congregation of the Free Reformed Church, a group which had broken away from the main Reformed Church of France. Concerned for church unity, he persuaded them to rejoin the main denomination. His writings include works on church history, some volumes of sermons which enjoyed wide popularity, and a liturgy, or order of worship, which was used by many French Reformed churches.

For Those Who Suffer

You are love,
and you see all the suffering,
injustice, and misery,
which reign in this world.
Have pity, we implore you,
on the work of your hands.
Look mercifully on the poor,
the oppressed, and all who are heavy laden
with error, labour and sorrow.
Fill our hearts with deep compassion for those
who suffer,
and hasten the coming of your kingdom of justice
and truth.

Dwight L. Moody

1837-1899

Dwight Lyman Moody left school when he was only thirteen to work in his home town in Massachusetts. At seventeen he moved to Boston and became an assistant in his uncle's shoe shop. Here he attended a Congregational Sunday school and was converted through the influence of his teacher. But for a whole year he was not admitted to membership of the church because he was so ignorant of basic doctrine!

He became a travelling salesman in the Chicago area and had considerable business success. But his heart was in evangelism. In 1860 he gave up his business for full-time Sunday school and youth work. He established a non-denominational church, and met Ira D. Sankey, who became his musical associate, composing hundreds of hymns which they used in evangelistic meetings.

At first Moody and Sankey met with little response, but their campaigns suddenly caught fire on their third visit to England, where it was estimated that over two-and-a-half million people attended their meetings. Back in the USA, Moody established boys' and girls' schools, and a Bible Institute. During his lifetime he is said to have covered a million miles on preaching tours and spoken to 100 million people.

Use Me

Use me then, my Saviour, for whatever purpose, and in whatever way, you may require. Here is my poor heart, an empty vessel; fill it with your grace. Here is my sinful and troubled soul; quicken it and refresh it with your love. Take my heart for your abode; my mouth to spread abroad the glory of your name; my love and all my powers, for the advancement of your believing people; and never suffer the steadfastness and confidence of my faith to abate; so that at all times I may be enabled from the heart to say, 'Jesus needs me, and I am his.'

Robert Louis Stevenson

1850-1894

'My fame will not last more than four years,' predicted Stevenson when his books started to become best sellers. But generations of readers have proved him wrong. 'Treasure Island', 'Kidnapped' and his other adventure stories are as popular as ever with both children and adults.

The son of a Scottish lighthouse engineer, Stevenson expected to follow his father into engineering but changed his studies to law and became an advocate. Suffering fron a chronic lung complaint, he travelled abroad for the sake of his health, and started to write travel books, essays and short stories. These were soon followed by his novels which were an immediate success.

Stevenson married a Californian divorcee whom he had met on his travels, and they settled in Samoa with her two children. Here he became a kind of honorary chief, gathering the Samoans around him to judge disputes or tell stories. This gained him the nickname 'Tusitala' — the 'teller of tales'. Though he had rebelled against the strict Calvinism of his upbringing, he still had a strong faith, and his prayers were written for Samoan converts. 'A generous prayer,' he said, 'is never in vain.'

Family Prayer

Lord, behold our family here assembled.
We thank you for this place in which we dwell,
for the love that unites us,
for the peace accorded us this day,
for the hope with which we expect the morrow;
for the health, the work, the food and the bright skies
that make our lives delightful;
for our friends in all parts of the earth.
Give us courage and gaiety and the quiet mind.
Spare us to our friends, soften us to our enemies.
Bless us, if it may be, in all our innocent endeavours;
if it may not, give us the strength
to endure that which is to come
that we may be brave in peril,
constant in tribulation, temperate in wrath
and in all changes of fortune
and down to the gates of death,
loyal and loving to one another.
As the clay to the potter
as the windmill to the wind
as children of their sire,
we beseech of you this help and mercy
for Christ's sake.

Evening Prayer

WRITTEN AND READ TO HIS FAMILY THE NIGHT BEFORE HIS SUDDEN DEATH

Go with each of us to rest; if any awake, temper to them the dark hours of watching; and when the day returns, return to us, our sun and comforter, and call us up with morning faces and with morning hearts, eager to labour, eager to be happy, if happiness should be our portion, and if the day be marked for sorrow, strong to endure it.

John Oxenham

1852-1941

Novelist and poet, William Dunkerley (who wrote under the name John Oxenham) was the son of a Manchester wholesale provision merchant. After travelling in Europe and the USA for his father's business, he took up writing full time and with Jerome K. Jerome started a magazine called 'The Idler'. In 1913 he published a book of verse, 'Bees in Amber', at his own expense as publishers thought it uncommercial; it sold a quarter of a million copies. His other works, including forty novels, were extremely popular during World War I. He was a devout Congregationalist but had great sympathy with the Roman Catholic church.

From
'A Little Te Deum of the Commonplace'

For all the first sweet flushings of the spring;
The greening earth, the tender heavenly blue;
The rich brown furrows gaping for the seed;
For all thy grace in bursting bud and leaf . . .
For hedgerows sweet with hawthorn and wild rose;
For meadows spread with gold and gemmed with stars,
For every tint of every tiniest flower,
For every daisy smiling to the sun;
For every bird that builds in joyous hope,
For every lamb that frisks beside its dam,
For every leaf that rustles in the wind,
For spiring poplar, and for spreading oak,
For queenly birch, and lofty swaying elm;
For the great cedar's benedictory grace,
For earth's ten thousand fragrant incenses,
Sweet altar-gifts from leaf and fruit and flower . . .
For ripening summer and the harvesting;
For all the rich autumnal glories spread —
The flaming pageant of the ripening woods,
The fiery gorse, the heather-purpled hills,
The rustling leaves that fly before the wind
and lie below the hedgerows whispering;
For meadows silver-white with hoary dew;
For sheer delight of tasting once again
That first crisp breath, of winter in the air;
The pictured pane; the new white world without;
The sparkling hedgerows witchery of lace,
The soft white flakes that fold the sleeping earth;
The cold without, the cheerier warmth within . . .
For all the glowing heart of Christmas-tide,
We thank thee, Lord!

Walter Rauschenbusch

1861-1918

Born to German immigrant parents in Rochester, New York, Rauschenbusch was educated in Germany and the United States. Converted to Christianity at seventeen, he studied for the ministry and became the pastor of a German-speaking Baptist church near Hell's Kitchen, a notorious slum area in New York. Here he was deeply moved by the situation of immigrants and the socially disadvantaged.

He carried this concern with him when he went to lecture in the New Testament and church history at Rochester Seminary. He has been called the 'father of the social gospel in America' — becoming so well-known through his writings that he was consulted by President Roosevelt on his party's social policies. He called himself a Christian Socialist, rejecting Marxism because it did not take into account man's sinfulness. A committed pacifist, he maintained, 'War is the most sinful thing there is.'

Thanks For Creation

O God, we thank you for this earth, our home; for the wide sky and the blessed sun, for the salt sea and the running water, for the everlasting hills and the never-resting winds, for trees and the common grass underfoot. We thank you for our senses by which we hear the songs of birds, and see the splendour of the summer fields, and taste of the autumn fruits, and rejoice in the feel of the snow, and smell the breath of the spring. Grant us a heart wide open to all this beauty; and save our souls from being so blind that we pass unseeing when even the common thornbush is aflame with your glory, O God our creator, who lives and reigns for ever and ever.

Karl Barth

1886-1968

'The deepest truth . . . can only be grasped by seeing man as he is in Christ,' wrote Barth. In his study and writings, he sought to recall the church to the fundamentals of Christian faith and experience.

The son of a professor of New Testament theology, Barth was born in Basle, studied in Switzerland and Germany and became a lecturer at various German universities. He wrote about 500 books and articles, of which the most important were his influential commentary on Paul's epistle to the Romans, and the unfinished 'Dogmatics' on which he worked for many years.

When the Nazis began to gain power, Barth was sacked from his teaching job. He had moved from a position of neutrality to an active involvement with the Confessing Church who openly opposed Hitler. Barth refused to take an oath of obedience to the Führer and was exiled to his native town, where he continued to teach and write to the end of his life.

At the Start of Worship

O Lord our God! You know who we are; men with good consciences and with bad, persons who are content and those who are discontent, the certain and the uncertain, Christians by conviction and Christians by convention, those who believe, those who half-believe, those who disbelieve.

And you know where we have come from: from the circle of relatives, acquaintances and friends or from the greatest loneliness, from a life of quiet prosperity or from manifold confusion and distress, from family relationships that are well ordered or from those disordered or under stress, from the inner circle of the Christian community or from its outer edge.

But now we all stand before you, in all our differences, yet alike in that we are all in the wrong with you and with one another, that we must all one day die, that we would all be lost without your grace, but also in that your grace is promised and made available to us all in your dear Son Jesus Christ. We are here together in order to praise you through letting you speak to us. We beseech you to grant that this may take place in this hour, in the name of your Son our Lord.

Reinhold Niebuhr

1892 -1971

A leading modern theologian, Niebuhr started his ministry as a pastor in the United Church of Christ in a Detroit industrial parish. He left there to join the staff of Union Theological Seminary, New York, where he continued to struggle with the issue of how a traditional Christian faith could be related to the modern world.

While working as a minister, Niebuhr had been a member of the Socialist Party but later broke away from it. Instead he committed himself to finding a middle way between Communism and what he saw as excessive American idealism. He founded two organizations — Christianity and Crisis, and Americans for Democratic Action — to work out from a Christian viewpoint a realistic approach to world problems and America's involvement in world affairs. As well as his political involvement, Niebuhr wrote seventeen major books on theology and social issues.

Discernment

O God, grant us the serenity
to accept what cannot be changed,
the courage to change what can be changed,
and the wisdom to know the difference.

Interdependence

O God, you have bound us together in this bundle of life;
give us grace to understand how our lives depend on the
courage, the industry, the honesty and integrity of our
fellow men; that we may be mindful of their needs,
grateful for their faithfulness, and faithful in our
responsibilities to them; through Jesus Christ our Lord.

Corrie ten Boom

1892-1983

The scene was the concentration camp at Ravensbruck. Corrie ten Boom stood naked with her sister Betsie, watching a guard beat a prisoner. 'Oh, the poor woman,' Corrie cried, meaning the prisoner. 'Yes, may God forgive her,' replied Betsie, meaning the guard. This attitude of forgiveness was to determine Corrie's life-work.

The two sisters had been arrested when it was discovered that Casper ten Boom, their watchmaker father, had been sheltering Jews in a secret room in their Amsterdam house as an expression of Christian love. The materials to build the room had been smuggled into the house in a grandfather clock!

Betsie died in Ravensbruck, but before she died she told Corrie of a vision God had given her: a home in which healing could be found for those emotionally and physically damaged by the horrors of the concentration camps. After her release Corrie made this vision a reality. But it was not only the victims she encountered. God enabled her to do the hardest thing of all — to forgive her former persecutors. Since World War II Corrie ten Boom has travelled all over the world spreading her message of love and reconciliation.

The Hiding Place

Thank you, Lord Jesus
that you will be our hiding place,
whatever happens.

Suffering

Lord Jesus, you suffered for me — what am I
suffering for you?

Casper ten Boom's Prayer
WHEN CONFRONTED WITH A WATCH HE COULD NOT MEND

Lord, you turn the wheels of the galaxies. You know what
makes the planets spin. And you know what makes this
watch run . . .

Prayers from the Third World
TWENTIETH CENTURY

The great missionary outreach of the eighteenth and nineteenth centuries meant that churches were established all over the world in countries where there had previously been very little or no Christian presence. Today many of those churches, especially in Asia, Africa and South America, are flourishing and developing their own styles of worship and church life. Now the movement has begun to reverse itself, as missionaries from the 'deprived' Third World countries help the declining Western church. Their enthusiasm and fresh outlook, as well as their awareness of their countries' pressing social problems, can be a spur to make us re-examine the effectiveness of our own faith.

Prayer of a Muslim Convert

O God, I am Mustafah, the tailor, and I work at the shop of Muhammed Ali. The whole day long I sit and pull the needle and the thread through the cloth. O God, you are the needle and I am the thread. I am attached to you and I follow you. When the thread tries to slip away from the needle it becomes tangled up and must be cut so that it can be put back in the right place. O God, help me to follow you wherever you may lead me. For I am really only Mustafah, the tailor, and I work at the shop of Muhammed Ali on the great square.

Prayer of an African Girl

O great Chief, light a candle within my heart that I may see what is therein and sweep the rubbish from your dwelling place.

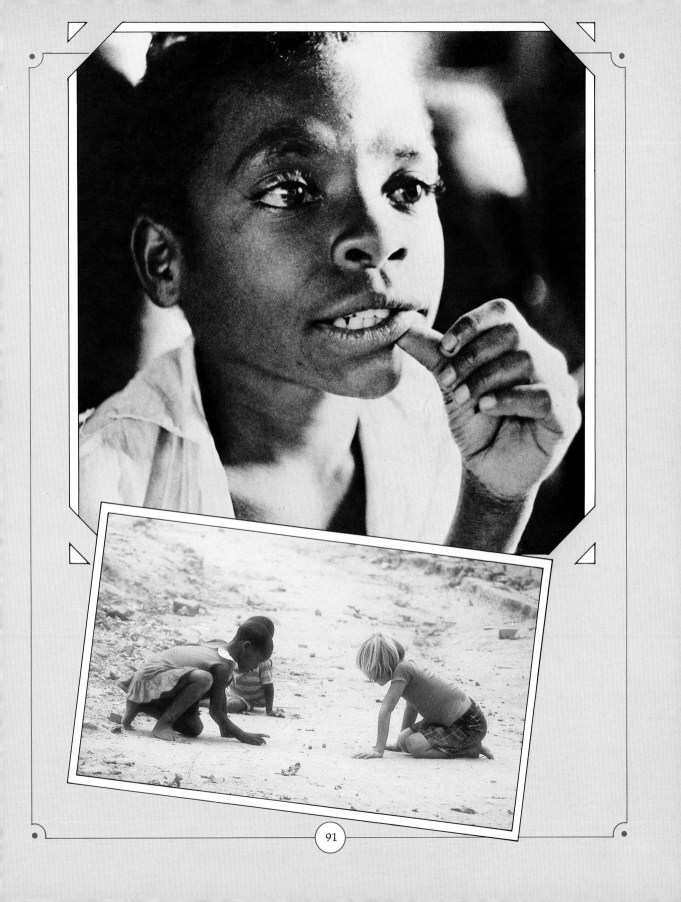

O Tree of Calvary
CHANDRAN DEVANESEN, INDIA

O Tree of Calvary
send your roots deep down
into my heart.
Gather together the soil of my heart,
the sands of my fickleness,
the stones of my stubbornness,
the mud of my desires,
bind them all together,
O Tree of Calvary,
interlace them with your strong roots,
entwine them with the network
of your love.

Nkosi Sikilel i Afrika
THE AFRICAN NATIONAL ANTHEM
TRANSLATED BY ADAM SMALL, A CAPE TOWN POET

Have compassion, Lord
upon this land.
Let your mercy
come upon it
Lord.
Hold your hands out
Lord
and bless this land
land that burns
Lord
land that burns.
Let our people stand
before you
all.
Judge them with
your judgement
hard, O Lord.
Let justice triumph
in this land
land that burns
Lord
land that burns.

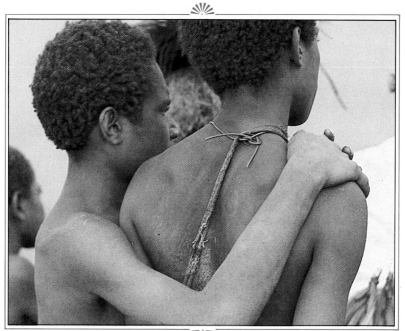

Prayer of a Xhosa Christian
SOUTH AFRICA

You are the great God — he who is in heaven.
You are the creator of life, you make the regions above.
You are the hunter who hunts for souls.
You are the leader who goes before us.
You are he whose hands are with wounds.
You are he whose feet are with wounds.
You are he whose blood is a trickling stream.
You are he whose blood was spilled for us.

A Chinese Woman's Prayer
AFTER LEARNING TO READ

We are going home to many who cannot read.
So, Lord, make us to be Bibles
so that those who cannot read the Book
can read it in us.

Alan Paton

BORN 1903

Alan Paton's famous novel, 'Cry the Beloved Country', is perhaps the best-known statement of what it means to live in South Africa under apartheid. It won awards as soon as it appeared in 1948, and has been made into an opera and a film.

A member of the Anglican church, Paton has been a teacher of maths, physics and English, and the principal of a reformatory. He has also worked in a tuberculosis settlement run by the charity Toc H. Since 1948 his main occupation has been writing both fiction and non-fiction. He is the founder and former president of the Liberal Party of South Africa, which was declared illegal by the Nationalist government in 1968. After a trip to the United States, he was deprived of his passport by the South African authorities. 'He believes,' says one commentator, 'that there is a road away from destruction, and he stakes out the signposts along the road.'

The Work of Peace

Give us courage, O Lord, to stand up and be counted,
to stand up for those who cannot stand up for themselves,
to stand up for ourselves when it is needful for us to do so.
Let us fear nothing more than we fear you.
Let us love nothing more than we love you,
for thus we shall fear nothing also.
Let us have no other God before you,
whether nation or party or state or church.
Let us seek no other peace but the peace which is yours,
and make us its instruments,
opening our eyes and our ears and our hearts,
so that we should know always what work of peace we
may do for you.

Dag Hammarskjöld

1905-1961

'Markings', Hammarskjöld's spiritual diary published after his death, was described by its author as 'a sort of white book concerning my negotiations with myself and with God'. Its discovery surprised many who had known only the public statesman and not the private individual.

Dag Hammarskjöld was the son of a Swedish prime minister. He studied law and economics, and after teaching political economy at the university of Stockholm, embarked on a civil service career. By 1951 he had been made deputy foreign minister. Two years later he was elected the second Secretary General of the United Nations. His approach to this role was that of a 'practical peacemaker'. As such he helped to stave off war in the Middle East during the Suez crisis of 1956. In 1960 he was denounced by the Soviet Union for sending a UN force to the troubled Belgian Congo. A year later he was killed in an air crash on a peace mission to that country. He was awarded a posthumous Nobel peace prize.

God the Artist

You take the pen
and the lines dance.
You take the flute,
and the notes shimmer.
You take the brush,
and the colours sing.
So all things have meaning and beauty
in that space beyond time where you are.
How, then, can I hold back anything from you?

Mercy and Justice

Almighty,
forgive my doubt,
my anger,
my pride.
By your mercy
abase me,
in your strictness
raise me up.

Dietrich Bonhoeffer

1906-1945

'Bonhoeffer was one of the very few men I have ever met to whom his God was real and close,' said an English officer who was imprisoned with him at Flossenburg in Bavaria. The son of a professor of psychiatry, Bonhoeffer grew up in an academic atmosphere. He studied theology at Berlin and in 1930 became a lecturer there. Within a few years Hitler had risen to power. As early as 1933, Bonhoeffer denounced the Nazi ideology in a radio broadcast. He spent two years in charge of the German congregations in London, urging them not to compromise with Hitler as the German church had done. Inevitably, in 1936 he was forbidden to continue lecturing.

Concerned that Christianity should mean getting involved in society, he gradually moved from a pacifist position to the view that a dictator like Hitler could only be overthrown by force. In 1943 he was arrested, implicated with his brother-in-law in a plot to assassinate Hitler. Two years were spent in various prisons where he stood out by his cheerfulness and care for others. On 8 April 1945 he held a service for his fellow-prisoners, 'finding just the right words' according to one of them. The following day he was hanged. 'This is the end,' he said as he was led out, 'for me the beginning of life.'

Morning Prayers

In me there is darkness,
But with thee there is light,
I am lonely, but thou leavest me not.
I am feeble in heart, but thou leavest me not.
I am restless, but with thee there is peace.
In me there is bitterness, but with thee there is
patience;
Thy ways are past understanding, but
Thou knowest the way for me.

Lord Jesus Christ
Thou wast poor
and in misery, a captive and forsaken as I am.
Thou knowest all man's distress;
Thou abidest with me
when all others have deserted me;
Thou doest not forget me, but seekest me.
Thou willest that I should know thee and
turn to thee.
Lord, I hear thy call and follow thee;
Do thou help me.

Archbishop Helder Camara

BORN 1909

'My personal vocation is that of a pilgrim of peace . . . I would prefer a thousand times to be killed than to kill.' In recognition of this attitude and its outworking, Helder Camara has been awarded four peace prizes including the Pope John XXIII memorial award, and has been given honorary doctorates by universities in America, France and Germany.

Archbishop of Olinda and Recife in his native Brazil, Camara has for many years been an active campaigner for social reform in the Latin American continent. In pursuing this aim he has enlisted the support of bishops in Brazil and other South American countries, organizing conferences to determine the church's task in furthering justice and peace. In spite of opposition from the Brazilian government he continues his work.

King's Son

Lord
isn't your creation wasteful?
Fruits never equal
the seedlings' abundance.
Springs scatter water.
The sun gives out
enormous light.
May your bounty teach me
greatness of heart.
May your magnificence
stop me being mean.
Seeing you a prodigal
and open-handed giver
let me give unstintingly
like a king's son
like God's own.

Mother Teresa of Calcutta

BORN 1910

'The biggest disease today is . . . the feeling of being unwanted,' says Mother Teresa. Treating this 'disease' is the aim of all her work. Born Agnes Gonxha Bojaxhiu to Albanian parents in Skopje, Yugoslavia, she volunteered for missionary work while still at school. In 1928 she was sent to Loreto Abbey in Ireland and then the following year to teach geography in a Calcutta girls' school.

In 1948 she felt called out of the security of the convent to work among the poorest of the poor — the Calcutta slum and street dwellers. With special permission from the pope she started a school for the street children, supported by donations only. Within a year she had been joined by several former pupils, who were the first Missionaries of Charity. In 1952 Mother Teresa picked up a dying woman from the street, half eaten by rats and ants. At once she set up the Home for the Dying in a former Hindu temple. Work among lepers followed, and the Missionaries of Charity spread throughout India.

Today there are over 100 centres of the Missionaries of Charity across the world from Britain to Australia, serving Jesus Christ and seeing him in the person of the very poorest.

Daily Prayer
USED BY WORKERS AT THE CALCUTTA ORPHANAGE

Dearest Lord, may I see you today and every day in the person of your sick, and, whilst nursing them, minister unto you.

Though you hide yourself behind the unattractive disguise of the irritable, the exacting, the unreasonable, may I still recognize you, and say: 'Jesus, my patient, how sweet it is to serve you.'

Lord, give me this seeing faith, then my work will never be monotonous. I will ever find joy in humouring the fancies and gratifying the wishes of all poor sufferers.

O beloved sick, how doubly dear you are to me, when you personify Christ; and what a privilege is mine to be allowed to tend you.

Sweetest Lord, make me appreciative of the dignity of my high vocation, and its many responsibilities. Never permit me to disgrace it by giving way to coldness, unkindness, or impatience.

And O God, while you are Jesus my patient, deign also to be to me a patient Jesus, bearing with my faults, looking only to my intention, which is to love and serve you in the person of each one of your sick.

Lord, increase my faith, bless my efforts and work, now and for evermore, Amen.

Carmen Bernos de Gasztold

'Prayers from the Ark' is a unique collection of prayer/poems, written from the point of view of animals but with a great deal to say about human nature. Most of them were written during the German occupation of France, when their author was scraping a living working in a silk factory. She wrote in a freezing bedroom, wrapped in an old eiderdown while the rest of her family huddled around the warm stove downstairs.

Carmen de Gasztold was born in Bordeaux, the daughter of a professor of Spanish who lived in constant poverty due to mental illness. Whenever things got too difficult the five children were sent away, and Carmen suffered deeply from this. At sixteen, after her father's death, she began to teach children privately, but was so shy that at first she walked round and round her pupils' houses, afraid to go in. Eventually teaching and a broken engagement led to a nervous breakdown. She was taken in by the nuns of the Abbaye at Limon-par-Igny, where she gradually recovered. She still lives there in a tower room which used to be a dove cote, writing, working in the library and fitting stained glass.

Prayer of the Ox

Dear God, give me time.
Men are always so driven!
Make them understand that I can never hurry.
Give me time to eat.
Give me time to plod.
Give me time to sleep.
Give me time to think.

Prayer of the Butterfly

Lord!
Where was I?
Oh yes! This flower, this sun,
thank you! Your world is beautiful!
This scent of roses . . .
Where was I?
A drop of dew
rolls to sparkle in a lily's heart.
I have to go . . .
Where? I do not know!
The wind has painted fancies
on my wings.
Fancies . .
Where was I?
Oh yes! Lord,
I had something to tell you:
Amen.

Thomas Merton

1915-1968

In 1941, instead of continuing in the career as a university professor of English for which his education in England, France and the United States had prepared him, Thomas Merton entered the Trappist monastery of Gethsemani in Kentucky to begin a life of silence. He was to spend the rest of his life there; but far from living a life of obscurity, he became in the opinion of many 'the most significant figure in American Catholicism'. His writings cover a wide range of subjects: Eastern and Western spirituality, radical politics, the 'desert fathers' of the early church, pacifism and the nuclear arms race.

This poem, which its author calls a psalm, could also be called a prayer in the sense of the old French peasant who, when asked what he did as he sat at the back of the church, replied 'I look at God, and he looks at me and we are happy.' It captures vividly the atmosphere of the life of a contemplative monastery.

The Reader

Lord, when the clock strikes
Telling the time with cold tin
And I sit hooded in this lectern

Waiting for the monks to come
I see the red cheeses, and bowls
All smile with milk in ranks upon their tables.

Light fills my proper globe
(I have won light to read by
With a little, tinkling chain)

And the monks come down the cloister
With robes as voluble as water.
I do not see them but I hear their waves.

It is winter, and my hands prepare
To turn the pages of the saints:
And to the trees thy moon has frozen
on the windows
My tongue shall sing thy Scripture.

Then the monks pause upon the step
(With me here in this lectern
And thee there on thy crucifix)
And gather little pearls of water
on their fingers' ends
Smaller than this my psalm.

Carl Burke

BORN 1917

'God is for real, man' and its sequels, which appeared in the late 1960s, were a new type of prayer book: prayers and meditations written for and by delinquent teenagers. They describe, often in their own slang, their search for God and their discovery of how God can change lives.

The books arose out of the experiences of their compiler, Carl Burke. As well as spending thirteen years as a Baptist minister in New York State, he has been a director of therapeutic camps for children at risk and those convicted of crime. Since 1963, he has served as chaplain of Erie County Jail and Children's Detention Home.

Searching

Do you know what it is like
To search for someone to love
and never find someone?

Why, O God,
Did it take this
To make me
Find myself?

Where have you been?
Where have I been?
Is it too late for me?
Is there still a chance?

Thinking With Everything

Dear God, make me think about what I'm doing
with my mind
with my body
with my habits
with my study
with my friends
with my hopes
with my parents
with my faith
with life.

Michel Quoist
BORN 1918

Since its publication in 1963, Abbé Quoist's 'Prayers of Life' has become one of the most popular and widely-used prayer books around the world. Its down-to-earth prayers reflect its author's two great interests: young people and the poor. Before submitting his thesis for a doctorate in social and political sciences, he lived in one of the poorest quarters of Paris to gain more knowledge of his subject.

Michel Quoist was for some time a parish priest in an inner-city area of his birthplace, Le Havre, and now works as a chaplain to youth groups and clubs in the city. His prayers, as their title suggests, are inspired by scenes of everyday life: bricklaying, a telephone conversation, a floodlit football match, a bald head. 'Nothing is secular,' he says in one of them, 'everything has been made sacred in its origin by God.'

My Friend

I shook hands with my friend, Lord,
And suddenly when I saw his sad and anxious face,
I feared that you were not in his heart.
I am troubled as I am before a closed tabernacle
when there is no light to show that you are there.
If you were not there, Lord, my friend and I would
be separated.
For his hand in mine would be only flesh in flesh
And his love for me that of man for man.
I want your life for him as well as for me.
For it is only in you that he can be my brother.

The Wire Fence

The wires are holding hands around the holes:
To avoid breaking the ring, they hold tight the
neighbouring wrist,
And it's thus that with holes they make a fence.

Lord, there are lots of holes in my life.
There are some in the lives of my neighbours.
But if you wish we shall hold hands
We shall hold very tight
And together we shall make a fine roll of fence
to adorn Paradise.

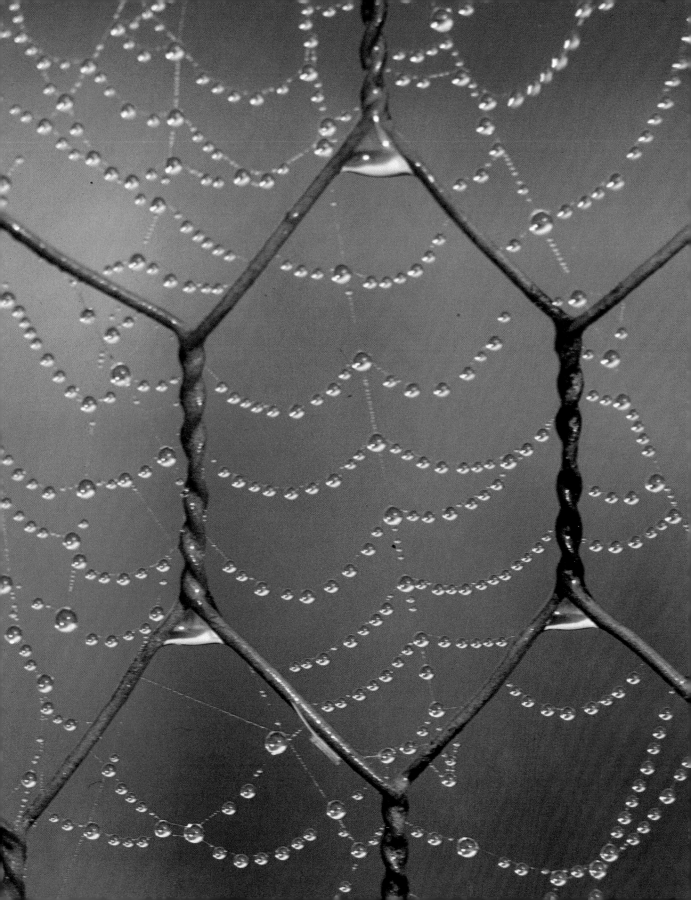

Henri Nouwen

BORN 1932

In 1974 Henri Nouwen spent seven months with the Trappist monks of the Abbey of the Genesee in New York, as a time of spiritual exploration. From his experiences there he wrote 'Genesee Diary', which has been hailed as a modern Christian classic. Five years later he went back to Genesee for a further six months, to go deeper into the life of prayer and contemplation. As a personal discipline he wrote one prayer a day, and a selection of those prayers were published as 'A Cry for Mercy'. 'My words are not more than the walls that surround a silent place,' says the author of these prayers. 'They hide the prayer of God, which can never be printed in a book.'

Born in Holland, Father Nouwen has made his home in America, teaching, lecturing and writing. After ten years on the staff of the Yale Divinity School of Pastoral Theology, he has now joined the community at Genesee.

The Difficulties of Praying

Why, O Lord, is it so hard for me to keep my heart directed toward you? Why do the many little things I want to do, and the many people I know, keep crowding into my mind, even during the hours that I am totally free to be with you and you alone? Why does my mind wander off in so many directions, and why does my heart desire the things that lead me astray? Are you not enough for me? Do I keep doubting your love and care, your mercy and grace? Do I keep wondering, in the centre of my being, whether you will give me all I need if I just keep my eyes on you?

Please accept my distractions, my fatigue, my irritations, and my faithless wanderings. You know me more deeply and fully than I know myself. You love me with a greater love than I can love myself. You even offer me more than I can desire. Look at me, see me in all my misery and inner confusion, and let me sense your presence in the midst of my turmoil. All I can do is show myself to you. Yet, I am afraid to do so. I am afraid that you will reject me. But I know — with the knowledge of faith — that you desire to give me your love. The only thing you ask of me is not to hide from you, not to run away in despair, not to act as if you were a relentless despot.

Take my tired body, my confused mind, and my restless soul into your arms and give me rest, simple quiet rest. Do I ask too much too soon? I should not worry about that. You will let me know. Come, Lord Jesus, come. Amen.

The Taizé Community
FOUNDED 1940

After the outbreak of World War II, Roger Schutz began to shelter Jewish and other refugees in a large house in Burgundy, not far from the ancient abbey of Cluny. In 1942 he was forced out by the Gestapo, but two years later he managed to return with three others to start a Christian community. In 1949 the first seven brothers pledged themselves to celibacy, obedience to authority and the sharing of all their property. Taizé is now an ecumenical community of over seventy members, including Franciscan and Eastern Orthodox monks. Brother Roger is its Prior.

During the summer months young people from all over the world gather to study and meditate at Taizé. This has led to the formation of a network of small cell groups all over the world who engage in social projects ranging from scientific research to dish-washing. A World Council of Youth has been formed to co-ordinate these young people's practical experiments in Christian living.

Simplicity and Joy
FROM THE RULE OF TAIZE

O Lord Christ, help us to maintain ourselves in simplicity
and in joy, the joy of the merciful, the joy of brotherly
love. Grant that, renouncing henceforth all thought of
looking back, and joyful with infinite gratitude, we may
never fear to precede the dawn, to praise and bless and
sing to Christ our Lord.

A Prayer For Reconciliation
BY BROTHER ROGER AND MOTHER TERESA OF CALCUTTA

O God the Father of all
you ask every one of us to spread
love where the poor are humiliated
joy where the church is brought low
and reconciliation where people are divided
father against son, mother against daughter
husband against wife
believers against those who cannot believe
Christians against their unloved fellow Christians.
You open this way for us,
so that the wounded body of Jesus Christ, your church,
may be leaven of communion for the poor of the earth
and in the whole human family.

Freed
BY BROTHER ROGER

O Christ,
you take upon yourself all our burdens
so that,
freed of all that weighs us down,
we can constantly begin anew to walk,
with lightened step,
from worry towards trusting,
from the shadows towards the clear flowing waters,
from our own will
towards the vision of the coming Kingdom.
And then we know,
though we hardly dared hope so,
that you offer to make every human being
a reflection of your face.

Make Us Servants
BY BROTHER ROGER

Lord Christ,
you remain, unseen,
at our side,
present like a poor man
who washes the feet of his friends.
And we,
to follow in your footsteps,
we are here, waiting for you
to suggest signs of sharing
to make us into servants
of your Gospel.

Coventry Cathedral Prayer

1964

On 14 November 1940, a German air-raid passed over the centre of England. The medieval cathedral was left a burnt-out shell. Because of the extent of its destruction, Coventry has become as familiar a name around the world as Dresden.

In 1962 a new building was consecrated. The cathedral has become a centre of reconciliation between former enemies. In the ruins stands an altar with a cross of nails and another made from charred timbers. Before this altar each lunchtime there is a short service which uses the litany below, first composed for an International Students' Festival held in February 1964, and written on a plaque in front of the altar.

Father, Forgive

The hatred which divides nation from nation,
    race from race, class from class,
Father, forgive.
The covetous desires of men and nations
    to possess what is not their own,
Father, forgive.
The greed which exploits the labours of men,
    and lays waste the earth,
Father, forgive.
Our envy of the welfare and happiness of others,
Father, forgive.
Our indifference to the plight of the homeless
    and the refugee,
Father, forgive.
The lust which uses for ignoble ends
    the bodies of men and women,
Father, forgive.
The pride which leads to trust in ourselves
    and not in God,
Father, forgive.

Short Prayers

'When you pray, do not use many words,' Jesus instructed his disciples. Christians have often taken this advice to heart, composing brief, straight-to-the-point appeals to God.

The Jesus Prayer

Based on the words of the blind beggar healed by Jesus, this prayer has traditionally been used as a basis for meditation by Eastern Orthodox monks.

Lord Jesus Christ, Son of God,
have mercy on me a sinner!

At the End of the Day

This prayer is one of the earliest Christian prayers recorded.

Be off, Satan, from this door and from these four walls. This is no place for you; there is nothing for you to do here. This is the place for Peter and Paul and the holy gospel; and this is where I mean to sleep, now that my worship is done, in the name of the Father and of the Holy Spirit.

Prayer For Protection

This inscription was found on a Roman house in Turkey.

May the Lord of the powers in his mercy protect us
as we go in and out.

Sir Francis Drake
1541-1596

This prayer is based on words that Queen Elizabeth I's great soldier and explorer used on the day he sailed into Cadiz in 1587 to fight the Spanish.

O Lord God, when thou givest to thy servants to
endeavour any great matter, grant us also to know that it
is not the beginning, but the continuing of the same to the
end, until it be thoroughly finished, which yieldeth the
true glory; through him who for the finishing of thy work
laid down his life, our Redeemer, Jesus Christ.

Sir Jacob Astley
1579-1652

A supporter of the king in the English Civil War, Astley spoke this prayer before the battle of Edgehill on 23 October 1642, the first major battle of the war, in which he was commanding the king's forces.

Lord, thou knowest how busy I must be this day.
If I forget thee, do not thou forget me.

William Penn
1644-1718

Expelled from Oxford University and imprisoned several times for his Quaker faith, Penn was a passionate defender of religious freedom. Because of a debt King Charles II owed to his father, he was granted land in America and there founded the state of Pennsylvania, a refuge for persecuted Quakers and a 'holy experiment' in religious community.

O Lord, help me not to despise or oppose
what I do not understand.

Bishop Stratford

DIED 1707

Often associated with John Wesley, this prayer was used by him but attributed to Bishop Stratford.

O Lord, let me not live to be useless!

Billy Bray

1794-1868

The story of the tin miner who was changed by his faith from a drunken, blaspheming good-for-nothing into an ardent evangelist is still legendary in his native Cornwall. He is said to have spoken this prayer while waiting with his fellow miners to begin the day's shift.

Lord, if any have to die this day, let it be me,
for I am ready.

General Gordon

1833-1885

'This earth hath borne no simpler, nobler man' said the poet Tennyson of Charles George Gordon. Famous for his military successes in China and the Sudan, General Gordon was an unorthodox but committed Christian who spent much time and money providing education and work for poor youngsters. He was killed in the siege of Khartoum.

O Lord God, grant us always, whatever the world may say, to content ourselves with what thou wilt say, and to care only for thine approval, which will outweigh all words.

Psalm 23 For Busy People
Toki Miyashina

Psalm 23, 'The Lord is my shepherd', has probably been set to music and paraphrased more than any other part of the Bible. This modern version from Japan gives it a new impact for twentieth-century readers — especially in the city.

The Lord is my pace-setter, I shall not rush;
he makes me stop and rest for quiet intervals,
he provides me with images of stillness,
which restore my serenity.
He leads me in the way of efficiency,
 through calmness of mind;
and his guidance is peace.
Even though I have a great many things to accomplish
each day

I will not fret, for his presence is here.
His timelessness, his all-importance will keep me
in balance.
He prepares refreshment and renewal
in the midst of activity,
by anointing my mind with his oils of tranquility;
my cup of joyous energy overflows.
Surely harmony and effectiveness shall be
the fruits of my hours
and I shall walk in the pace of my Lord,
and dwell in his house for ever.

Blessings and Doxologies

Just as friends often want to say something significant when they part, such as 'Look after yourself', so it seems to be natural for Christians to have special sayings to repeat at the end of worship. A doxology is a short prayer of praise to God, used either at the close of a service or at the end of a particular section of the service. Early church leaders such as the apostle Paul also included doxologies in their letters to the churches. A blessing is addressed to the worshippers but also indirectly to God, asking him to continue giving the good things he has promised to his people.

Both doxologies and blessings have been used throughout the church's history, and as the example from Martin Luther King shows, they are still being composed today.

'The Grace'
2 CORINTHIANS 13:14

May the grace of the Lord Jesus Christ,
and the love of God,
and the fellowship of the Holy Spirit,
be with you all.

A Doxology From Paul
EPHESIANS 3:20-21

Now to him who is able to do immeasurably more than
all we ask or imagine, according to his power that is at
work within us, to him be glory in the church and in
Christ Jesus throughout all generations, for ever and ever!
Amen.

Songs of Praise From 'Revelation'

You are worthy, our Lord and God,
to receive glory and honour and power,
for you created all things,
and by your will they were created and have their being.

Worthy is the Lamb, who was slain,
to receive power and wealth and wisdom and strength
and honour and glory and praise!

To him who sits on the throne and to the Lamb
be praise and honour and glory and power,
for ever and ever!

Amen!
Praise and glory
and wisdom and thanks and honour
and power and strength
be to our God for ever and ever.
Amen!

An Egyptian Doxology
THIRD CENTURY

May none of God's wonderful works
keep silence, night or morning.
Bright stars, high mountains, the depths of the seas,
sources of rushing rivers:
may all these break into song as we sing
to Father, Son and Holy Spirit.
May all the angels in the heavens reply:
Amen! Amen! Amen!
Power, praise, honour, eternal glory
to God, the only Giver of grace.
Amen! Amen! Amen!

A Traditional Blessing

Based on the opening verse of Psalm 67, this blessing has been repeated since at least the seventh century before Christ, and has passed into use in the Christian church.

The Lord bless us and keep us, the Lord make his face to shine upon us, and be gracious unto us, the Lord lift up the light of his countenance upon us and give us peace.

Blessing of the Cheese and Olives
SECOND OR THIRD CENTURY

Sanctify this milk that has been pressed into cheese, and press us together in charity. Grant that this fruit of the olive-tree may never lose its savour; for the olive is a symbol of that abundance which, at your bidding, flowed from the tree and is there for those who trust you.

A Hymn From the Greek Church

Praise is your due,
hymns are your due,
glory is due to you, Father,
Son and Holy Spirit,
due to you always.
Amen.

Thomas Ken

1637-1711

A popular hymn-writer and author of devotional works, Ken was Bishop of Bath and Wells in south-west England, and a chaplain to King Charles II. Under King James II he was imprisoned in the Tower of London with six other bishops, and when he refused to swear an oath of allegiance to William and Mary was deprived of his bishopric.

Blessing and honour, thanksgiving and praise
more than we can utter be unto thee,
O most adorable Trinity, Father, Son and Holy Ghost,
by all angels, all men, all creatures
for ever and ever Amen and Amen.
To God the Father, who first loved us,
and made us accepted in the Beloved;
To God the Son who loved us,
and washed us from our sins in his own blood;
To God the Holy Ghost,
who sheds the love of God abroad in our hearts
be all love and all glory for time and for eternity. Amen.

Martin Luther King

1928-1968

King first became involved with the black civil rights movement while working as the pastor of a Baptist church in Montgomery, Alabama. Influenced by the tactics of Gandhi in India, he engaged in non-violent action such as bus boycotts and marches, and a drive to encourage black Americans to register as voters. His actions led to two important Civil Rights Acts.

In 1968 he was shot dead in Memphis by a white gunman. This blessing was spoken to his congregation in Montgomery as he left them to devote all his time to political action.

And now unto him who is able to keep us from falling
and lift us from the dark valley of despair to the bright
mountain of hope, from the midnight of desperation to the
daybreak of joy; to him be power and authority, for ever
and ever.

Index of Subjects

Entries relate to main topics of prayers, not necessarily to titles.
Some prayers appear under more than one heading.

Index of Authors

Acknowledgements

*The following prayers are copyright and are
included by kind permission of the copyright holders*

Bible prayers from The Holy Bible, New International Version © 1978 by New York International Bible Society, first published in Great Britain in 1979.

'The Wish of Manchan of Liath' and 'Christ's Bounties' from *A Celtic Miscellany* by Kenneth H. Jackson, reprinted by permission of Routledge and Kegan Paul Ltd.

Anselm, 'Desire For God' and 'A Call to Meditation' reprinted by permission of Penguin Books Ltd from *The Prayers and Meditations of St Anselm* by Benedicta Ward.

Amy Carmichael, 'It Is Not Far' reprinted by permission of The Society for Promoting Christian Knowledge from *Edges of His Ways* by Amy Carmichael. For USA: reprinted by permission of Christian Literature Crusade from *Edges of His Ways* by Amy Carmichael.

Corrie ten Boom, 'The Hiding Place', 'Suffering' and 'Casper ten Boom's Prayer' from *Each New Day With Corrie ten Boom*, reprinted by permission of Kingsway Publications Ltd. For USA: from *Each New Day* by Corrie ten Boom. Copyright © 1977 by Corrie ten Boom. Published by Fleming H. Revell Company. Used by permission.

'Prayer of a Muslim Convert', 'Prayer of a Xhosa Christian' and 'A Chinese Woman's Prayer' reprinted by permission of the Church Missionary Society from *Morning, Noon and Night* by John Carden.

Alan Paton, 'The Work of Peace' reprinted by permission of Seabury Press, New York, from *Instrument of Thy Peace* by Alan Paton.

Dag Hammarskjöld, 'God the Artist' and 'Mercy and Justice' reprinted by permission of Faber and Faber Ltd from *Markings* by Dag Hammarskjöld, translated by W. H. Auden and Leif Sjoberg. For USA: reprinted by permission of Alfred A. Knopf Inc. from *Markings* by Dag Hammarskjöld, translated by W. H. Auden and Leif Sjoberg.

Dietrich Bonhoeffer, 'Morning Prayers' reprinted by permission of SCM Press Ltd from *Letters and Papers From Prison* by Dietrich Bonhoeffer, enlarged edition 1971. For USA: reprinted by permission of Macmillan, from *Letter and Papers From Prison* by Dietrich Bonhoeffer.

Mother Teresa, 'Daily Prayer' reprinted by permission of William Collins and Company Ltd from *Something Beautiful for God* by Malcolm Muggeridge. For USA: reprinted by permission of Harper and Row Publishers Inc. from *Something Beautiful for God* by Malcolm Muggeridge.

Carmen Bernos de Gasztold, 'Prayer of the Ox' and 'Prayer of the Butterfly' reprinted by permission of Macmillan, London and Basingstoke, from *Prayers From the Ark* by Carmen Bernos de Gasztold, translated by Rumer Godden. For USA: reprinted by permission of Viking Penguin Inc. from *Prayers From the Ark* by Carmen Bernos de Gasztold, translated by Rumer Godden.

Thomas Merton, 'The Reader' reprinted by permission of Sheldon Press from *The Collected Poems of Thomas Merton*. For USA: reprinted by permission of New Directions Publishing Corporation from *The Collected Poems of Thomas Merton* copyright © 1949 by Our Lady of Gethsemani Monastery.

Carl Burke, 'Searching' and 'Thinking With Everything' reprinted by permission of William Collins and Company Ltd from *Treat Me Cool, Lord* by Carl Burke, published by Fount Paperbacks. For USA: reprinted by permission of the National Board of Young Men's Christian Associations in the USA from *Treat Me Cool, Lord* by Carl Burke.

Michel Quoist, 'My Friend' and 'The Wire Fence' reprinted by permission of Gill and Macmillan Ltd, from *Prayers of Life* by Michel Quoist. For USA: reprinted by permission of Andrews and McMeel Inc. from *Prayers of Life* by Michel Quoist.

Henri Nouwen, 'The Difficulties of Praying' reprinted by permission of Gill and Macmillan Ltd, from *Cry for Mercy* by Henri J. M. Nouwen. For USA: reprinted by permission of Doubleday and Company Inc. from *Cry for Mercy* by Henri J. M. Nouwen. Copyright © 1981 by Henri J. M. Nouwen.

Prayers from Taizé, 'Simplicity and Joy', 'A Prayer For Reconciliation', 'Freed' and 'Make Us Servants' reprinted by permission of A. R. Mowbray and Company Ltd.

'Father, Forgive' reprinted by permission of Coventry Cathedral.

Credits

Photographs: Robin Bath, page 14; BBC Hulton Picture Library, pages 37, 72, 80-81; Bibliothèque Publique et Universitaire de Genève, page 47; British Library, page 24; British Tourist Authority, page 112; Chichester Cathedral Enterprises, page 31; Mary Evans Picture Library, pages 27, 29, 39, 43, 44, 45, 52, 56, 77, 79, 83, 111; Sonia Halliday Photographs: F. H. C. Birch, page 25, Sister Daniel, pages 46, 100, 105, Sonia Halliday, pages 18, 23, 36, 50, 66-67, Jane Taylor, page 99; Robert Harding Picture Library, page 92; Kupferstichkabinett, Basle, page 41; Lion Publishing: David Alexander, pages 13, 17, 42, 58-59, 71, 74-75, 97, 102, 114-15, Jon Willcocks, pages 10, 19, 20-21, 34, 61, 84, 116 and endpapers; Mansell Collection, pages 48, 54, 55; David Morgan, page 60; Popperfoto, page 122; Jean-Luc Ray, pages 91, 93; Master and Fellows of Sidney Sussex College, Cambridge, page 32; Derek Widdicombe, page 26; Nicholas Servian FIIP/Woodmansterne, pages 108-9; ZEFA, pages 73, 85, 89, 98, 118-19 and cover.

Drawings on pages 12, 53, 87, 94 are from *1800 Woodcuts by Thomas Bewick and his school*, edited by Blanche Cirker, © Dover Publications Inc.; those on pages 11, 57, 59, 65, 69, 78 are from *Handbook of Early Advertising Art* by Clarence P. Hornung, © 1956 Dover Publications Inc.

The cartoon on page 103 is by Papas, copyright © 1967 William Collins and Sons.

The Tower of London, page 121, is taken from an engraving by Stanislaus Holler.